Uncharted WATERS

Navigating Life in the Supernatural

BRAD BONNER

I dedicate this book to my wife, April Lane Bonner. She is full of love, integrity, and mercy. She loved me at my worst, and she has continued to love me as God is transforming me. She has taught me so much about unconditional love. She embodies what a godly wife, mother, and friend is. I am incredibly fortunate to live life with you and our kids. April, I love you more than I can express.

Contents

Introduction

My wife and I were on a dinner date at a steakhouse in Dothan, Alabama. After enjoying an amazing fillet steak, we were on our way out the door and heading to the movies. A sixty-year-old woman slowly passed by us using a walker, and we could tell she was struggling. When we got to the car, I asked my wife if she noticed the woman. She nodded, and I told her, "I'll be back in a few minutes."

With one mission in mind, I headed back inside the restaurant to find the woman and to see Jesus transform her life.

I located the woman and her family at a booth. The woman was on the inside part of the booth hemmed in by her husband, and across from her sat her two sisters. As I knelt beside the table, I noticed the walker folded up and leaning against the wall. After telling them my first name, I asked the lady why she had to use the walker. She told me she'd had three strokes, two back surgeries, had bad hips, and the list continued. I already had all the information I needed for her to be healed—Jesus is King, and He paid the price for us to be made well.

The woman's sisters were uncomfortable with me being there and wanting to pray, but that did not slow me down. I am continually captivated by God's love, and their offense was not nearly enough to stop me from allowing God to alter their sister's life right there in that restaurant. I reached across the table and asked the lady to give me her hand. As she did, the power of God engulfed the woman in the booth.

I prayed a brief prayer, commanding her body to be healed in Jesus' name. The woman looked at me in stunned disbelief as intense heat began flowing through her back and down her legs. I told her that Jesus was healing her and that she might want to try walking without her walker at some point that day. She immediately elbowed her husband to move so that she could get out to walk. Her sisters frantically tried to reason with the woman not to get up. The lady would not consent, as the transforming fire of God was now burning inside of her.

She began walking without her walker as happy tears flowed down her cheeks and wonder lit up her face. She looked as if someone had hit the fast-forward button on a remote control as she picked up speed in the aisle. All the pain was gone from her back and legs! As she walked, the only thing she felt was intense heat and the love of God.

She praised God as the walker stayed folded up against the wall. Her sisters and husband were speechless as they watched her walking unassisted and without any pain. I was overjoyed as I watched another life get radically altered as the goodness of God touched her. The husband reached over and gave me a great big hug as tears filled his eyes. The two sisters were amazed to witness the power of God, and they both wanted me to pray with them. Everyone present encountered the love and presence of Jesus that day in the steakhouse. After this, my wife and I enjoyed the rest of our date.

Days like this await all of us as believers in Jesus.

Chapter 1: My Story

This is my story of how Jesus came and rescued me. I was born to two young, newly married college students. They loved me, their only child, with great brilliance. I was the only grandchild on both sides of the family for nearly eighteen years. I had loving family supporting me all my life. I grew up in a Pentecostal church and had the financial resources to do most anything I wanted. Also, I had success academically and athletically. I really lacked for nothing. However, I was not immune to making mistakes and taking lumps growing up. I had broken bones, fights with friends, and traumatic breakups with girlfriends.

Around my senior year in high school, I began to drink alcohol. I was arrested as a minor in possession of alcohol right before I went to college. It scared me straight for a couple of days, and two weeks later I was off to Georgia Southern University in Statesboro. I made many new friends and many new memories—some good, some bad, some horrible. All the while God was watching over me, though I had all but forgotten my upbringing. I was living life in the fast lane: excessive parties, loads of alcohol, various experiments with party drugs, and numerous girls.

The Descent

For the first three years of college, I was on top of the world. I prized my friends, popularity, success in school, and most of all, the parties and girls. Nevertheless, when I turned 21, everything began to change for me. I began to be awfully depressed. Nothing in the world seemed to make me happy any longer. No matter how many parties I went to, how many friends or girls I hung out with, or how many sports games I attended, it all became repetitive. I was so distraught that I left Statesboro midsemester.

Around midnight on a weekday, I headed out toward Texas to visit my cousin, Dave Whittaker. I did not even bother withdrawing from my college courses, nor did I notify my friends, roommates, or parents. I received zeroes that semester on my work, which shocked my family and friends. Dave, my cousin, was one of my best friends. It also helped that he is an amazing listener, trustworthy, and brilliant. He has a PhD in psychology. He tried to help me make sense of things. He did all he could, as he has always been an incredible friend to me. But, I did not get any peace or comfort from the drive out to Texas or my time there.

I ended up driving back to my parents' house in Donalsonville, Georgia. They were confused by my actions, and disappointed as well. I reentered college the next semester, and again I quit midsemester.

This time I decided to end my life. When I left Statesboro, I had no plan. I packed a few of my belongings and all my cash and drove off in the middle of the night. I was scared, lonely, and utterly, despondently depressed. I started heading north. I was drinking alcohol and driving, all while being bombarded with suicidal thoughts. I spent one night in Virginia. I pondered jumping off one of the high bridges and meeting my demise. I had such dreadful agony in my heart. I hated myself, my life, my failures and mistakes. I loathed people. I was livid. I thought if there were a God, I despised Him most of all.

I decided—spur of the moment—to shave my head and join the military instead of killing myself. I went and took the Armed Services Vocational Aptitude Battery, or ASVAB, test. After completing the test and spending time with the recruiter, he told me I could join the following day. After another night of heavy drinking, I decided not to show up and join the military; instead, I headed out toward the mountains.

Deeper into Darkness

I ended up in Cherokee, North Carolina. I remembered that at some point growing up, my parents had taken me there on vacation. I figured I could end my life in the solitude of the mountains. I was drinking huge amounts of alcohol at this point, mainly liquor. I found a cheap motel and paid for a week in advance. I would listen to the most melancholy music of the day and drown my existence away in a drunken stupor. I discovered a casino in that town, and I began to play blackjack during the day.

Eventually, after almost two weeks on my own, I was down to $700, and I had no contact with anyone other than Dave, who I called from pay phones. I can't imagine the hell that my parents, grandparents, and friends were going through. They had no clue where I was or how to get in touch with me. My family was in constant prayer for me. My mother and grandmother, especially, were warriors in the prayer realm on my behalf.

I was so belligerent one night that I decided to break my silence and call Dave from my hotel room. He was able to track me down, and in the middle of the night, he called my parents and told them where I was. My dad, grandfather, and a police friend of my father's took off in the middle of the night to try and reach me before I could leave. Around 8:00 a.m., I was awakened by a knock on my hotel door. I was shocked to open the door and see my dad standing there. I had never had such a reality check as I did then, hungover and sick, standing in my boxers, surrounded by alcohol in a strange hotel room in North Carolina. As I stood face-to-face with my dad, my next surprise was seeing my grandfather and Mr. Ray, the policeman, outside in the vehicle. Dad helped me gather up my things and told me we were going home.

They had driven over six hours to find me. He gave me a trash bag to dry heave into. I slept most of the time in the car. I was embarrassed, irritated, sick, and overly miserable the whole drive.

To my surprise, I awoke to find they had taken me to a behavioral health crisis facility in Thomasville to get help. I thought to myself,

This is a place for people with mental illnesses or addictions ... not someone like me.

Abruptly, I was immersed in a place of insanity. I was encircled by scary people. The place was horrifying. I quickly made up my mind that I would lie to the doctors and tell them a plausible story. When I was taken in to see the head psychiatrist, I told him I wanted to be an actor and most of what I had done had been an act. I told him I was unsure what I wanted to do in life. I informed him that my family was mistaken and worried only because they misinterpreted the reason I quit college and went to quietly reflect in the seclusion of the mountains. I told him of course I had been drinking some, but I was twenty-two years old and just blowing off some steam.

I presented a convincing story and turned on as much personality and charm that I could. It worked. The doctor believed me and told me I had no business being there at the facility. He arranged for me to leave immediately.

My mom and dad came to pick me up a couple hours later. As soon as we arrived in Donalsonville, I packed my things and headed back to Statesboro. I began carousing with my friends and looking for a job. I told my friends that I had hit a rough patch but I was okay now. The normal life I hoped to resume was short-lived. A few weeks later, I was extremely drunk one night and somehow managed to get in a fight with three active military guys. They broke my nose and beat me up pretty bad. My face was battered. I drove back to Donalsonville to be with my parents because I was embarrassed and ashamed of who I was, and I did not really know where else to go. My parents welcomed me in.

A couple days later, they went out to eat, and I stayed at home. I was sober, yet dying on the inside. The pain of living another moment was too great for me to endure. I knew my dad had a pistol in the house for protection. I retrieved it, sat on their staircase, gave the middle finger to the world, and said f*#$ this life. I put the gun to my temple and my finger on the trigger. Before I could pull the trigger, I began to violently shake, and I started weeping. Little did I know, God's great love and mercy would not let me end my life. He loved me too much. The prayers of my family were too powerful for darkness to overtake me.

I remember being so angry at myself for not being able to go through with pulling the trigger. I angrily put the gun back in its place, and a couple of days later, I headed back to Statesboro to move back in with my friends.

Trying to Fill the Void

I worked a few different jobs, but I was finally hired at a locally owned sandwich shop. After a few months of working there, we hired a young, beautiful girl to serve tables. This girl, April, would become a great friend.

We began dating, and within one month we were already talking about getting married. Soon after, we found out she was pregnant, and we decided to go ahead and get married. April made me so very happy. I loved being around her as much as I could. I thought to myself, *Wow, this is what I have been missing! Now I can be happy. A wife, and a child on the way.* However, no one can fill the void of not being in a relationship with God.

After a few months, the drinking was worse than ever and I was depressed all over again. I started playing more and more poker, and got good enough to play professionally, mostly online, for over three years. While sober, I made decent money doing this. The problem was, at night I was constantly drunk and would then get online and blow loads of the money that I had earned while sober by playing blackjack and poker at higher limits against harder competition.

I would leave my wife several times a year and fly to Las Vegas to play live poker against people who did not know what they were doing. Another benefit of playing in Vegas was that most of these bad players would be getting drunk, which worsened their play. However, by the end of most nights, I would be drunker than them all and lose the money I made during the day. I would also leave my wife and go to the mountains to drink and be alone. I lived quite a terrible life and put my wife through pure hell.

Depression and suicidal thoughts were a constant in my life. The ups and downs of variance in playing poker contributed to my depression. One night I sat down with over $3,000 at a $25/$50-pot-limit Omaha game online: real cash. I was drinking heavily and playing against several well-known pros. By 3:00 a.m., I had over $15,000 in play on the table. One of my good friends was watching me online. He called me on the phone, begging me to get up and leave the table. He knew I was very drunk and would be well-served to wake up the next day with a clear head and preserve my money. However, I ignored him and continued in my stupor. In three hands' time, I went bust and lost over $15,000. I went into a rage.

Later, severely depressed, I told my wife about losing the money and had a huge fight with her. In my drunkenness, I called my parents at 8:00 a.m. and told them I was divorcing April. There were many times we almost divorced; but my wife, ever full of mercy, always wanted to believe the best in me.

The second year of our marriage, I agreed to see a psychologist to get help. I met with a wonderful guy in Statesboro. I was diagnosed with bipolar disorder. I was manic depressive, frequently had suicidal thoughts, and I had substance abuse problems. He prescribed different medications and would adjust them monthly. After a year of treatment, I did not really feel any better, so I stopped taking the medications and stopped seeing the doctor.

Disintegration

In 2006, I re-enrolled in college and I graduated in the summer of 2007 with a BBA (bachelor of business administration) in management. The weekend of graduation, my wife went to visit her mom for the weekend. I was partying with my friends. Around 2:00 a.m., I was at the point of blacking out, but I drove my car to get a pizza. I passed out at the wheel.

Next thing I know, I'm in my bed with cops standing over me and putting me in handcuffs. I had totaled my graduation present from my grandfather—a new car—by smashing into another vehicle. Somehow, I managed to drive my car home even though it was totaled. My wife and child had to pick me up the next day in jail. I had only driven my graduation gift for about a week, and now the lawyer bills and fines were going to pile up. I also got sued by the family that I hit in the accident.

God showed me great mercy. I could have died that night. I could have killed that entire family that night. Thankfully, none of them were physically hurt. I had minor burns on my face from the airbag. I avoided any additional prison time by serving lots of community service and losing my driver's license for six months. However, I continued drinking, and I continued playing poker for a living.

April graduated from Georgia Southern University with a teaching degree in 2009. My family, amazing as they are, provided great benefits for us. My grandfather and grandmother purchased a home for us, right next door to them in my hometown of Donalsonville. My father, then superintendent of the school system, interviewed my wife through all the proper channels, and she aced the interviews. She was hired to teach eighth grade, and has been teaching successfully and with much joy for the past eight years.

January 20, 2010, I celebrated my twenty-ninth birthday with my family at my parents' house. By this time, our daughter Cadance was five years old, and we had been back in my hometown for over eight months. My grandmother, Helen Dick, gave me a birthday card containing a check for $100, a picture of khaki pants, and a note from Granny saying, "Hope you use some of this money to purchase a pair of pants and wear them to church." I told my grandmother that I would plan on using the money, but certainly not for dress pants and that she would not see me at church. The events that followed this birthday party would forever alter my life.

The Phone Call

A week after my birthday, I decided to head down to Biloxi, Mississippi, and play some live poker. This would give me a break from grinding out poker online, and I could drink at night without disturbing my wife and child. My third day there, I received a life-changing phone call from my aunt. It was around 10:00 a.m., and I knew something was not right, as my aunt and I almost never talked on the phone.

With trepidation, I answered. My aunt was sobbing and screaming simultaneously, "They are gone, they are gone, they are gone." Through the utter chaos coming from her vocal cords into my ear, my heart sank. I was able to gather from her that an automobile accident had occurred and some of my loved ones had died. She hung the phone up suddenly and I began panicking.

I called my wife, Dad, Mom—anyone who may have their phone on while at work. I knew my daughter had spent the night with my ten-year-old cousin Ansley, my aunt's only child. They were staying with Granny Helen. I was in a rage of anger, mixed with despair at the thought of losing my only child. I just knew my five-year-old daughter was dead, along with Granny and Ansley.

Finally, I talked with Dad. He reassured me that, thankfully, my daughter had already been returned home before the automobile accident. My relief was short lived, as Dad then told me the crushing news that Granny Helen had died in the accident along with my precious cousin Ansley.

I packed my things and began the drive home, going way too fast, but fortunately I arrived safely and without a speeding ticket. At the funeral, I was numb. It all seemed unreal. My Granny and Ansley lying there on display, lifeless, yet I had just spent time with them only a week or so earlier. I believed there was no God, and I believed people just simply died. How hopeless and sad to live that way.

The next few days, I withdrew from people, even my wife, more than normal. I was drinking all day and night. I was contemplating life and how I would ultimately end my life and be free from this misery once and for all. February 8, 2010, was a Monday morning, and I was severely hung over after watching the Saints beat the Colts in the Super Bowl. My wife was already at work, and my daughter was at kindergarten. I woke up groggy and with a severe headache. I thought perhaps I might vanish off to Las Vegas or Biloxi, or possibly the mountains. I thought perhaps this might be my final day on earth, as I might also go through with ending my life. In a way, I would die that day, but not at all like I could ever imagine.

The Encounter

I sat on my couch in my living room around 9:00 a.m. I decided to have a brief chat with a God I didn't even know if I believed in. I was so sad and hurting inside. I said these words out loud, "God, if you are real, I need you."

Instantly, there in my living room, God came and rescued me! I began to shake and weep, as pure love began to emanate inside of me and on the outside of me. God covered my entire being; every cell experienced His presence. The Bible states, "God is love" (1 John 4:8). I experienced true love that day. I cried so hard that I could not believe I had that many tears inside of me. I was shocked at how powerful His love and presence felt.

During this encounter, I had no doubt God existed. I told Him, "I'm sad all the time. Can you take away depression?" Instantly, I felt this huge weight lift off me and I could breathe. I was free, and joy flooded my soul! God healed me completely of bipolar disorder. I have not had any medicine since and the suicidal thoughts ceased.

Later I said, "Lord, I'm so sorry I have wasted my life and been so angry with you, myself, and everyone else. Forgive me." I had an overwhelming urge to go and find a Bible. I knew we would have one somewhere in our house. I found an old King James Version, and I opened it and turned to the book of Matthew. I began to read the letters in red, as I knew enough to know Jesus spoke those words. I cried all the more—happy tears—as Jesus revealed Himself to me. He saved me.

I had wanted to die that day, and I did. The Bible says in 2 Corinthians 5:17, "Therefore, if anyone is in Christ, he is a new creation; old things have passed away; behold, all things have become new." It also states in Galatians 2:20, "I have been crucified with Christ; it is no longer I who live, but Christ lives in me; and the life which I now live in the flesh I live by faith in the Son of God, who loved me and gave Himself for me."

After an hour or more of encountering Christ's love and mercy, I called my dad. I told him I had great news. He was baffled to hear the tone of my voice, as I usually only called with bad news. I told him I had just gotten saved and encountered the Lord. Dad was filled with amazing joy, and soon my mother was notified as well.

Parents, don't give up on your lost children. My parents prayed for my salvation for over thirteen years, and the Lord has more than answered their pleas and cries for their son. In Luke 15, Jesus told a story of a prodigal son returning to his father. This story is very similar to my story.

Later that afternoon, my wife and daughter arrived home. My wife never knew what to expect from day to day living with me. Some of her thoughts would be, "Will Brad be drunk when I get home? Is Brad going to be home, or in a distant city? What mess am I going to encounter?" These were the type of questions harassing my wife each day after work. However, on this day she would receive life-changing news.

She opened the door and saw me. She looked very closely at me, and then she began to scan the house. She said, "What's different; what happened today?" I had not even said a word as she walked in, yet April was aware the entire atmosphere of the house, as well as my countenance, had changed since she had seen me last.

I told her, "I gave my life to King Jesus today." The power of God nearly knocked her over at the weighty presence of my words. The full weight of what she knew must be real began to settle in on her. She was overwhelmed with awe and wonder at all that had taken place in less than twenty-four hours. My wife and I embraced each other like two people reunitiing after years apart, and the tears of overwhelming joy began to flow. As I started to describe my life-changing encounter with Jesus with passion that had been missing from my life for years, April listened with amazement in her eyes and an immovable smile on her face.

As we talked, my wife revealed another sign and wonder that happened on this glorious day. She told me she had been cleaning her room at school. As she got behind one of her cabinets, she noticed a card behind it. The card was from Granny Helen to April when she had graduated college last summer. It was a voice-recordable card. Granny Helen's recorded voice message said, "I just wanted to say that we love you and can't wait for y'all to come home." Wow! The day I got saved, April found a card from my loving Granny who was always telling me about God's love and praying for me. Talk about a cloud of witnesses to the life of faith (Hebrews 12:1)!

I believe those who have gone on before us are very involved in rooting us on. I believe we are all one family and those who have gone on before us have passed the baton, yet they know our great reward is all interlocked together as the family of God. Not only were the holy angels celebrating on this day I had come home (Luke 15:10), but I believe those who have gone on before me to glory were allowed to experience God's goodness that day as they witnessed my salvation. On February 8, 2010, I was born again in Christ Jesus.

My outlook on life became very different. I was suddenly hungry to read the Bible. I began to attend church regularly. The urge to drink alcohol was gone. I was learning to live life sober; however, I drank alcohol occasionally after getting saved. The difference now was it really bothered me to drink. Also, I seemed to no longer be able to get drunk. Finally, on July 4, 2010, I drank alcohol for the last time in my life.

I was visiting some family and drinking with them to celebrate the Fourth in Florida. That night, I could not get drunk, and I felt the conviction of my Friend, the Holy Spirit. The next morning while reading the Bible in the bathroom, I said, "Holy Spirit, if you will give me the grace, I promise you this day that I will never let alcohol touch my lips again." Well, I'm happy to say that since July 5, 2010, I have been completely alcohol-free and have not slipped. All the glory to Jesus, as the Holy Spirit has provided great grace for me to live free.

There were times during the first couple of years where I was tempted to give in on occasion, but God's grace was always there for me and He gave me a way of escape to keep my promise to Him (1 Corinthians 10:13). For the first few months of my salvation, I still played online poker, but God began to deal with me on that issue as well. A couple of months into my journey with Christ, I decided to give poker up for the Lord. So, it was time for me to find another job, which was not easy in a small town.

Chapter 2: Life of Public Power

I briefly worked a couple of jobs before becoming a substitute teacher for a semester at the local school system. I did my best, but I was consistently asking the Lord what He wanted me to do for a living. In January 2011, a new restaurant opened in town. I was hired the day I was interviewed by the owner for the manager position.

I faced many new challenges, but the Lord helped me through them all. I interviewed and hired employees and set up credit card accounts to allow us to take that form of payment. I created marketing ideas and implemented them. The owner and I became very close and we worked well together. I constantly told my coworkers about Jesus and how He had saved me. I told them how Jesus healed people.

The "Crazy" Restaurant Manager

I had no idea how many miracles I would witness at this restaurant over the next couple of years. Many people would have their lives impacted in powerful ways because of the goodness of God. My coworkers were kind to me and listened, but when I was not around they would discuss that they thought I was crazy for believing this way, no matter how nice I was to them. I prayed for several people each week at work—usually customers with canes or wrist braces. I watched the presence of God touch many of them. I would constantly tell customers and employees testimonies of what I had seen God do. Then I would offer to pray with them to see what God would personally do for them.

I was at work on a Friday in 2011 around 5:30 p.m. I had noticed a young guy who lived nearby who was limping terribly. He was coming down the road from the restaurant I manage. He had been in this condition for over two weeks and did not look any better. I went outside and asked the guy if I could pray for his knee. He looked at me like I was crazy and said, "No thanks." He told me his knee was busted up badly. I began to tell him how awesome the God is that I serve, and after a couple of minutes the guy looked at me and said, "If you think your prayer will do any good, you go ahead and pray for me." I laid my hand on his knee and commanded the pain to leave in Jesus' name as I told the guy how much Jesus loved him.

I walked back into the restaurant and discovered all the employees had secretly gathered around to watch me go outside and pray. When I opened the door, they scattered to appear as though they were not watching. While dining, several customers had also paused to observe what was taking place. I calmly walked back inside while keeping a watchful eye on the guy, who was standing outside, looking very perplexed.

He slowly began to turn his hurt knee back and forth. Then he began to slowly squat all the way to the ground on his hurt knee. After testing it out a couple more seconds, this guy's face lit up like a little kid's on Christmas morning. He burst into the restaurant and shouted, "Dude, dude, my knee doesn't hurt. The pain is gone!" This guy started jumping up and down in the middle of the restaurant. Everyone was staring in total shock because we had all seen the terrible condition of his knee the past two weeks. My employees were as excited to witness this miracle as I was. Customers' mouths were agape as the guy started to jog around the restaurant. While all this was happening, I had my hands raised and I was praising Jesus out loud.

One of my employees in the kitchen who saw Jesus heal this guy's knee asked me if I thought God would heal her knee, too. I told her that God is no respecter of persons (Acts 10:34; Romans 2:11), and if God would heal that guy's knee then God would certainly heal her knee as well. We prayed right there in the kitchen, and God healed her knee too! The next day, she told me she had slept pain-free that night for the first time in months. Her knee remains pain-free to this day and hasn't given her any more problems.

You see, God doesn't desire for us to confine ourselves within the four walls of our churches and expect people to come to us. He wants you and me, His sons and daughters, to be willing to share His love and His goodness in public for all people to see (1 Peter 2:9). For it is not God's will that any should perish, but that all people repent (2 Peter 3:9). It is up to us to share the good news about Jesus Christ, our risen Savior, everywhere we go.

The following morning at work, the man who had his knee healed showed up with his wife. She asked me, "How did you do that? How did you make my husband's knee well?" Miracles point to Jesus. I responded, "I have a relationship with the King of all kings. He is the Son of God. His name is Jesus. He has given His friends the power to reveal His glory through miracles, signs, and wonders whenever we step out in faith. The Holy Spirit is present and releases the power of God through our lives. So, I partnered with the Holy Spirit for your husband to be healed, as Jesus commanded us in Matthew 10:8 to heal the sick. Now I get the privilege to tell you guys about the Kingdom of Heaven." I prayed with the couple for salvation.

His wife proceeded to tell me she had been looking everywhere for a job. We live in a very small town—it has just two traffic lights—with very limited opportunities to find work. She asked me if God could get her a job, just like He had made her husband's healing available. I told her He sure could. "With God all things are possible" (Mark 10:27). I prayed with her and told them I would see them soon.

The following day, the couple excitedly returned to see me. She told me she had gone to eat in a restaurant with her mother on the day I prayed with her. After eating their meal, the young lady visited the restroom. The owner of the restaurant came over to their table and asked her mother, "Does your daughter need a job?" The young lady was hired on the spot.

How awesome is God's love for us, His children? They had not said a word to the owner, yet the Holy Spirit prompted him to go over to their table. This young couple with a child on the way got blasted continuously by God's love for them.

Appointments with the "Real Jesus"

One morning before I went into work, a friend called and told me about a teacher at the high school who needed a miracle from the Lord. So, at 10:30 a.m., a friend and I went to his wife's classroom to meet Rhonda, the teacher in need, during their planning period. Rhonda had been saved and baptized at age seventeen, but at this stage in her life Rhonda was not showing the fruit of having a relationship with Jesus. She was searching for an authentic encounter with the real Jesus. She needed the real power of God, not just an idea or theology.

Rhonda had been to a doctor about a physical problem she had, and he had recommended surgery as the answer. She was very uncomfortable with that solution, so she sought a second opinion. She was going in for that second opinion on Friday, but Jesus got to her first. We told Rhonda a few testimonies about Jesus healing people and that we believed God wanted to heal her right there at the school.

After sharing the testimonies with her, I asked Rhonda if we could lay our hands on her shoulders to pray for her. As we began to pray, the power of the Holy Spirit began to rest upon Rhonda. Her body got hot as fire as the power of God came upon her, and she began to sway and almost fell to the ground. We were very excited about what God was doing right then and there. It is a wonderful feeling when you know without a doubt that God is right there with you as His presence begins to be evident.

Rhonda called my friend's wife that afternoon to tell her what was revealed by the second doctor she went to see. The doctor told her that what she had needed surgery to repair had shrunk, and she no longer required surgery. God had healed her just like we'd asked, and now Rhonda had no doubt that Jesus was very real and that He loved her very much. Two days later, on Sunday, Rhonda rededicated her life to Jesus. But that is not all. On Monday, she started a prayer group at school because she had the revelation that our God heals and that he hears our prayers. That is what salvation is all about.

The Greek word for salvation is *sozo* (see Romans 10:9). It means to be restored to a right relationship with God the Father. It also means to be healed, or made whole completely. We humans are made up of a spirit, a soul, and a body. So, to be made whole, Jesus wants to heal us spiritually (right relationship with Him through forgiveness of sin). He wants to deliver us emotionally (soul; our mind, will and emotions). Also, He wants to make us whole in body (physically made whole, healed of all sickness, disease, and torment). Rhonda experienced *sozo*, or salvation, completely. She was restored into right relationship with God, her body was healed, and her lifestyle reflected that she had had a real life-changing encounter with an awesome God. The fruit of what God was doing in her life was evident and still is evident in her life as she continues to be a powerful witness for Jesus Christ.

One day while managing the restaurant, a man I have known for many years came in to eat. Patrick had been fly-fishing about five years earlier and had an accident. The accident left his back in terrible shape and left him with nauseating pain. He went to the doctors, and they told him his back was so messed up that even if they did surgery, there was only a fifty-fifty chance they could repair his back and alleviate the pain. Patrick elected to not have surgery and he had terrible pain for over five years. In fact, many days Patrick had to use a cane to assist him in walking. He could not ride very far in a car without stopping and getting out because the pain in his back was so excruciating.

It was around forty degrees outside the day I had the opportunity to pray with Patrick at my workplace. He was wearing a shirt and jacket. I told Patrick I had witnessed Jesus heal many people, and I believed Jesus wanted to heal him right there, today. We went outside to pray and as we were about to begin, Patrick's mother-in-law and father-in-law pulled up. I asked them to come over and pray with us. I laid my hand on his back and commanded his back to be made whole and the pain to leave in Jesus' name, and then I gave God thanks.

As I turned to leave, Patrick told me to stop. He asked me to show him my hand. Curious, I asked him why. He said, "Because there is heat where you laid your hand, and it is still there." I told him God was healing his back and that was the reason he felt heat on that cold day. Amazed, Patrick came back into the restaurant to sit with his family. The heat of God continued to stay on his back for the next thirty minutes or so while his family ate.

All the pain in his back was gone, and God completely healed Patrick's back on that incredible day. I remember being so excited for him as he encountered the presence and healing touch of God sitting in a restaurant. Patrick is now able to check his own mail. He enjoys the walk down his driveway to the mailbox. He can lift heavy objects and walk around.

It has been several years since God healed him. He rides motorcycles and people who know him often ask if he had the surgery done to repair his back. He smiles as he recounts the day God healed him at a restaurant in his hometown. Many of his friends ask him if he is joking. However, he assures them that he is completely serious and thankful for what God did that day.

Releasing His Presence

As God's children, everywhere we go we have the ability to release His presence into the atmosphere around us. Luke 17:21 teaches us that "the Kingdom of God is within you." Mark 16:17 states that miraculous signs will follow those who believe in Jesus. So everywhere I go, I know that signs will follow me because I belong to Jesus. Whether I am at work, eating out, enjoying football games or church—wherever I may be, Jesus is with me.

One day while out to eat with my wife and two children, the owner of that restaurant came over to speak to us and to see Gabby, my youngest daughter at the time. As the owner talked with us, the Holy Spirit made me aware of His presence. I could sense His presence so strong that it was almost overwhelming. He gave me a word of knowledge (see 1 Corinthians 12:8) for the owner as she stood beside our table. He told me He wanted to heal her right shoulder.

Now understand, this woman did not have a sling or any other physical tip-off that her right shoulder was messed up. I waited until she walked away from our table, and then I told my wife and children about the word of knowledge that God had just given me. I also told them God was about to heal the lady.

I walked over to her and told her God loved her very much and that He wanted to heal the pain in her right shoulder. The woman's exact words to me were, "How do you know that? How could you possibly know about my right shoulder?" I told her that God knows everything about her and that He wanted her to encounter Him there in her restaurant. She then told me that she had had surgery on her right shoulder a month earlier and that the pain was terrible. I asked her if I could pray for her right then, because God was about to heal her.

I prayed a simple prayer over her shoulder and commanded the pain to come out in Jesus' name. The presence of God was amazing in that place. I asked the woman to move her shoulder around and see what she felt. She was astounded because all the pain was instantly gone! I gave her a hug and went back to eat my food.

We then watched the excited lady tell her cooks to stop cooking and the waitresses to stop working, and she called her husband over to her. She began to show them how her shoulder was completely pain-free, and she pointed over to our table and said, "That guy told me the exact spot on my body where I have pain and he prayed in Jesus' name and all the pain is gone!" She was excited, to say the least.

Several minutes later, this precious lady came over and just wanted to talk about Jesus. She was so grateful for what God had just done for her and for His presence which was so amazing inside her restaurant. Remember, I didn't know this lady. All I knew about her was that she was the owner of the restaurant. She only came over to our table to see my twenty-one-month-old daughter, Gabby. However, if we allow God, He will speak through us to everyone around us, no matter where we are or what we are doing.

God paid such a high price for every single person. God bankrupted Heaven by giving Jesus for you. You were worth it to God. God desires fellowship with you so much that He was willing to allow Jesus to go to the cross in your place that you might be reconciled to Him. For God so loved the world.

Jesus became love for us all. He was just like His Dad: perfect love (1 John 4:8). Jesus wants us to become love. When we love others and expect nothing in return, we start to become more like Jesus. He went to the cross for everyone out of radical love. Jesus went to the cross even for those who hung Him up there. Jesus gave His life for those who mocked Him, cursed Him, tortured Him, and killed Him. He laid down His life freely. He said, "Greater love has no one than this, than to lay down one's life for his friends" (John 15:13).

One busy Thursday night (we always had all-you-could-eat shrimp on Thursdays), I was overflowing with the joy of the Lord. I went to this big table of people in the back of the restaurant and began to share testimonies of different things I'd seen God do. I then asked a man in a wheelchair if I could pray for him. He told me he had a stroke almost eight years earlier and he hadn't been able to rehabilitate because he had terrible pain in his hips. So, I prayed for him, and the power of God manifested upon him.

After he got in his vehicle, the man's wife came back in the restaurant and told me I needed to get outside to see her husband. He was doing the twist in his truck and praising God because he had no pain in his hips at all. He was turning his body every which way and testing out his hips. Over the next few weeks, the man continued to experience no pain, and he was able to walk. He even walked at his church on a Sunday morning, and he continues to get stronger.

We are Made for More

Sadly, people have reduced being a Christian down to saying a prayer and getting to go to heaven when they die. But being a Christian is so much more. God calls us to be Christlike, walking in love and power just as Jesus did. When someone is born again, their lost identity as a son or daughter of God is restored. That means God literally takes up residence in a person's heart. He or she is prime real estate for the King of Kings (1 Corinthians 3:16).

One sunny summer day, I was at the ballpark watching Cadance, my eldest daughter, play baseball. I noticed a lady with a young child who had had various problems since his birth. I walked over to her and asked her if I could hold her baby and pray for him. She said yes, so I asked the Holy Spirit to touch the child. He had been born with one kidney smaller than the other, and this kidney was not healthy. The doctors told the mother that there was no medicine or procedure they could perform to make the other kidney grow and become healthy. The child would have health problems for the rest of his life. After I prayed, the mom took him to the doctor for another checkup. They discovered both kidneys were the same size and they were working properly. This happened many months ago, and the child's kidneys are still working well.

Many churches in our area have food drops, where underprivileged people can receive boxes of food. I enjoy helping at these different events from time to time. The pastor asked me to pray with the people who were stopping by for food. I met a young lady whose mom was dying of cancer and all her organs had shut down. The mom was given only a couple of days to live. We prayed and the presence of God in the room was amazing.

I went back to the food drop the following month to help and pray again. The young lady showed up, and when she saw me she ran up to me with tears streaming down her face and gave me the biggest hug. The very day we prayed for her mom, all her organs began working miraculously. In addition, her mom had stunned the doctors even more because she was in complete remission. Her mom was doing very well, and we just celebrated the goodness of God and thanked Him there at the food drop.

His Triumph, Our Freedom

In 1 Corinthians 2:4–5, Paul writes: "And my speech and my preaching were not with persuasive words of human wisdom, but in demonstration of the Spirit and of power, that your faith should not be in the wisdom of men but in the power of God." The prophet Isaiah spoke of Jesus before He was even born and declared what He would suffer on the cross for us. Isaiah 52:13–14 states: "Behold, My Servant shall deal prudently; He shall be exalted and extolled and be very high. Just as many were astonished at you, so His visage was marred more than any man, and His form more than the sons of men."

Wow—Jesus freely laid down His life for us. He was brutally beaten and tortured as the skin was violently ripped from His body. Blood poured out from His beaten body for you and me before He even was put on that rough, rugged, wooden cross. Jesus hung naked and beaten beyond all recognition on that cross for you and me. He purchased freedom from sin, sickness, disease, poverty, and addiction.

Before Jesus gave up His spirit on the cross, He declared, "It is finished!" (John 19:30). Jesus meant what He said. He has purchased the complete, finished work of redemption for mankind. It is settled. "Having wiped out the handwriting of requirements that was against us, which was contrary to us. And He has taken it out of the way, having nailed it to the cross. Having disarmed principalities and powers, He made a public spectacle of them, triumphing over them in it" (Colossians 2:14–15). Complete and total victory is Jesus Christ's alone. And because He lives and breathes inside of us, we are victorious as well because of what Jesus has done.

Knowing and believing this in my heart, I set out for Tallahassee, Florida, early one morning before I was to be at work. My cousin had called me the night before to tell me her stepmother was not doing well. This lady had undergone a knee replacement and had developed an infection. She was put on a ventilator and was not doing well at all. So, I set out to go and pray for her in the intensive care unit at one of the hospitals in Tallahassee. My cousin met me there and took me to the ICU room that her stepmother was in. I began to pray, and the presence of God instantly filled the room.

My cousin and I began to cry as we became acutely aware of the manifest presence of God. God is so truly wonderful and kind! After praying, I visited with my cousin for a few minutes before I began my trip home to try to make it to work on time.

Thirty minutes after leaving the hospital, I got a call from my cousin. She said, "You are not going to believe this." I told her to try me, because I know God is amazing. My cousin is a registered nurse and very knowledgeable about many medical things. She proceeded to tell me that her stepmother was being taken off the ventilator only thirty minutes after I had prayed with her. All her vitals and breathing were miraculously getting stronger and returning to normal. My cousin told me she had never seen anything like this and was so thankful for what she had just witnessed. All of this happened many months ago, and my cousin's stepmother is still doing well.

Miracles like this are available to everyone who believes in Jesus, because the Holy Spirit dwells within us. Romans 8:11 says that the same Spirit that raised Jesus from the dead, lives within us. Jesus is with us, and He desires to display the power of God through you … if you will only believe.

Divine Interruptions

One evening, we received an unanticipated knock on the door during family dinner time. A young lady stood expectantly at the door, wanting prayer. She and her husband had been trying to get pregnant for years without any success. April and I prayed for her womb to open and for life to come in. A couple of weeks later, the young lady and her husband came to see me at work. They were both smiling and crying with tears of joy, as they had just learned she was pregnant. Now, they have a beautiful, healthy, four-year-old daughter.

Several days later after receiving the couple's excellent news of the pregnancy, I was on my way to pick up my daughter from day care when I noticed a lady leaving a local restaurant with a knee brace on. So, I turned my car around and headed back towards the stop light. I parked my car on the other side of the street and ran through traffic just in time to catch up to the lady getting into her car.

I knocked on her window and she rolled the window down, smiling at me and saying, "I don't know you." I smiled back and told her that I noticed the knee brace she was wearing and that I believed God would heal her knee if she would let me pray for her. The lady smiled at me again and said, "I would be glad for you to pray for my knee." She went on to tell me that she had ligament damage in her knee and that it had bothered her for years. So, I commanded the swelling to go away and the pain to leave, and I thanked God for brand-new ligaments.

About a week later, I received a call from that lady. She said she had been looking for my phone number because she had to tell me what happened. The day I prayed for her knee, all the swelling and all the pain left. She has not worn the knee brace since I prayed for her. She cleans houses for a living and she is constantly bending and squatting—and she still has no pain in the knee.

We do most of our shopping in Dothan, Alabama. They have a variety of grocery stores, a mall, and best of all: great restaurants. After filling a shopping cart with groceries, I walked up to the cash register. I engaged in conversation for a moment with the cashier and the man bagging groceries. I asked them if they wanted to hear some good news (the gospel). They said, "Sure." I responded with something like this: "Jesus loves you so much. He paid the price that you might live."

As I walked away, the man bagging groceries called out to me, "You know, I think that might just be good news." So, I walked back over to the man and asked him if I could pray for him. He looked at me a little bit like he wasn't sure what prayer was, but he said yes nonetheless. I laid my hand on the guy's shoulder and I welcomed the Holy Spirit to make His presence known to the guy. The man began to cry right there at the counter as the love of God filled his life and he encountered Jesus. Who could imagine such a simple act of faith, like sharing the good news for thirty seconds with strangers at the counter in a grocery store, would lead to this man encountering the love of God. That guy will never be the same again because he encountered the presence of Jesus.

Going about my business, I received a call on my cell phone from an unknown number. The man's voice on the other end of the line told me he was from Cairo, Georgia. We had never spoken before. He heard from a mutual friend about some of the miracles I was seeing. After sharing a couple testimonies with him, he asked if I could come to Cairo to pray for his son. I said I would love to, and the following Saturday I went to see the man and his son.

His son's name was Brady, and he was about twenty-five years old. Doctors had discovered a huge growth on one of Brady's ribs. I could see it protruding from his rib cage. The doctors told him he needed surgery and they might have to remove his rib. The recovery time would be several months. We talked for a few minutes, and I quickly realized that

33

Brady was a brilliant young man. He was very scientific in his thinking and not so sure about God's existence, let alone that God does miracles.

We were in the shop that the family owned, and it was quite cold in that place. I began to tell Brady, his dad and mom, and Brady's fiancée about some of the miracles I have seen. I then told Brady the fire of God was about to touch him and he would not have to wonder whether God was real. I placed my hand on his side, and we prayed. I felt tears begin to drop on my arm as Brady began weeping. After praying for him, I spoke to Brady's mom and addressed several things with her.

About five minutes later, Brady interrupted us and said, with tears still filling his eyes, "Am I imagining this, or am I pouring sweat down my back? I feel like I am on fire." This skinny, young guy lifted his shirt in this very cold shop, and he had massive beads of sweat running down his back. He looked as though he had just completed a marathon run. The fire of God continued to burn inside of him for about thirty minutes. Obviously, after this amazing encounter with the presence of God, Brady had no more doubts about God's existence. I continued to speak with and pray for Brady's parents for a while afterwards. It was an amazing day.

About two weeks later, I got a call from those folks in Cairo. Brady had gone in for his pre-op appointment. The doctors discovered that the massive growth on Brady's rib had shrunk so much that it was almost nonexistent. They told them there was no need for the surgery and Brady could resume all his normal activities with no need for worry.

Jesus Goes to School

One of my favorite experiences with the Holy Spirit happened at the middle/high school in my hometown. Business leaders in the community were invited to attend an annual meeting to discuss different things the administration was doing to help kids get the most out of their education and also get parents more involved with the kids. As a manager of a restaurant, I was invited as well. The meeting was mostly composed of teachers, with a couple of members of the public, like me, there.

As I was listening to the discussions, the Holy Spirit began to speak to me about what He wanted to do. He told me there were at least two people in the meeting with severe back pain and He wanted to heal them. Now get this—there were only about fifteen total people present.

There was one lady who came to the meeting ten or fifteen minutes after it had started. As she walked through the door, the Holy Spirit highlighted her and let me know that she was one of the people with severe back pain. I didn't even know this teacher's name, but I knew what the Holy Spirit had just communicated to me. So, at the end of this forty-five-minute meeting, the person in charge asked if anyone had comments or questions. It was "do-or-die" time.

I had been so nervous waiting for this moment. I decided to trust the Holy Spirit and jump out in faith. I raised my hand and said, "I think all of you guys are doing an amazing job. Now, can I tell you something else?" Of course, the person in charge nodded her head. I continued with something like this: "God loves each person here so very much. He just told me there are at least two people in here with severe back pain, and He wants to heal them."

As I said this, I pointed to the woman the Holy Spirit had highlighted and told her, "And you are one of them." One man in the meeting immediately raised his hand and said he had terrible back pain and doctors were discussing putting metal rods in his back. The people in the room were astounded at what began to take place in this public setting.

I walked over to the man and prayed for him briefly. I commanded his back to be restored, and the man felt heat moving in his back. The pain left immediately as God healed his back. I then went over to the lady I had pointed out, and she was amazed that I knew about her back problems. She told me her name and that only three other people even knew about all the back problems she was having. I then told her that everyone in the room now knew about her back problems, but that everyone was also going to watch God heal her back of all pain right there.

She had been sleeping on the floor many nights because the pain was so bad. The doctors wanted to put metal screws into her back, but she was trying to put off the surgery because she enjoyed scuba diving. The surgery and metal screws would prevent her from scuba diving. I prayed for her, and God healed her too.

This meeting had nothing to do with God; it was a school meeting about school policies. But Jesus will show up anywhere at any time if we are willing to trust Him and do what He says.

After God healed these two amazing people, other teachers began asking for prayer. I got to pray for them and then tell everyone in the room about Jesus and how much He loves each of them. The gospel was on full display in public.

These two teachers have subsequently had their surgeries canceled and are both pain-free. The man was able to stop taking the powerful pain meds he was on. The lady has now been able to sleep at night in her own bed and no longer has to miss any work due to back issues.

About a year after that meeting, the male teacher who had been healed learned about a serious issue one of his students was having. The teacher asked him if he would like for me to come and pray with him and told the student how he had been healed. The young man agreed, and I went to see him for a couple of minutes.

He was having severe chest pains and had gone to the emergency room. An EKG was given and blood work was done. The doctor believed from the results that his left ventricle was blocked and the fifteen-year-old needed to be seen at the children's hospital as soon as possible in Birmingham. For the next couple of days, the young man continued to have problems and felt weak. He told me about his heart and the doctor's report and said he was scheduled for further tests in Birmingham the next day. I told him how much God loved him and that I believed God was about to totally heal him. I gave thanks to God for the young man, and then I commanded his heart and ventricle to work properly in Jesus' name.

The next day, I received an exciting call from the teacher. The young man had just called from Birmingham with the new test results. The EKG and blood work showed no problem: only a healthy heart! Also, the young man stated that after I prayed with him, he felt totally normal and he hasn't suffered any more weakness or pain.

The Great Physician

One Sunday afternoon, one of my coworkers at the restaurant told me that her daughter had pink eye. She said only a certain type of medicine can get rid of pink eye, and she would have to take her daughter to the doctor in the morning. I told this young lady that if she would let me pray with her, God would heal her daughter and no medicine would be needed. She agreed to let me pray with her. We prayed, and I asked the Holy Spirit to heal her daughter's eyes when the mom laid hands on her daughter after getting home. The mom did it when she got home, and she said, "Do it, God. Thanks, God."

The next morning, the family got up ready to go to the doctor. As the mom woke up her daughter, she expected crud to be around her eyes and for them to be looking the same as the past couple days due to the pink eye. She woke her daughter up and saw that there was no crud in her eyes; they were both completely crystal clear! The mom was so excited, and so was her mother-in-law, who had been babysitting while the mom was at work. The grandmother knew about the pink eye too, and she also witnessed God's power.

That afternoon, they told me about her daughter's eyes being healed and shared that the grandmother was having terrible knee problems. She was wearing a brace and could barely walk. She had already been to the doctor, and they told her the only way they could repair her knee was to break her kneecap and reset it. Ouch! However, the grandmother asked if I would come pray for her knee, because she had just witnessed the miracle with her granddaughter. So, I shared the gospel with the grandmother that afternoon and prayed for her knee. Within two weeks, her knee was totally healed and she was walking completely normal and pain-free. What a wonderful option, as opposed to having to break the kneecap and reset it.

A woman in the book of Matthew, chapter 9, suffered bleeding for over twelve years. She went to the doctors and spent lots of money to get well, but they could not help her. Jesus, however, healed her because she grabbed hold of the fringe of His garment. Her faith let power flow from Him into her situation.

I had another coworker who shared with me that her twenty-something daughter was suffering with bleeding as well. She had seen a doctor who wasn't able to do much about it. She also saw a specialist and got different opinions. They were unable to regulate her, and the bleeding problems continued. Her daughter came to the restaurant one afternoon, and I got to pray with her. That day, the bleeding stopped immediately. It has been over three years since this miracle, and the young lady has not had any more issues.

Freedom from Torment

A few months back, I received a phone call before work one morning from a nurse. Her husband's rotator cuff had been bothering him for a while; I had prayed for him at the restaurant's cash register, and God completely healed the man. Knowing this, the nurse told me that they had a guy at the hospital who the medical staff had been unsuccessful in helping. The doctors were not even sure what was causing his problems. She asked if I would be willing to come and pray for the guy, who was a family friend of hers.

I got ready as quickly as I could and headed to the hospital. When I entered the room, I found a horrendous site indeed. This grown man was writhing around in his hospital bed in immense pain. There was bile and vomit all over the place. I had never found myself in a situation quite like this one.

The man's father was in the room with him, and we talked for a couple of minutes. The dad said this had been going on for almost a week and the doctors were unable to help him. The dad also told me this had been happening off and on for over five years and that all kinds of tests had been run on his son to try and discover the cause.

As this grown man thrashed about in his bed, I went over and laid my hand on his stomach the best I could. I prayed for a minute, and nothing happened. I told the dad that I had to go to work and after work I would come back and pray for the man again.

As I got back to my car to leave, the Holy Spirit spoke to me. He told me the man had a tormenting spirit and that I was to command it to leave in Jesus' name. Wow! I had never had the Holy Spirit tell me this before.

I marched myself right back into the hospital and explained to the dad what the Holy Spirit had just told me. The dad did not have a clue what I was talking about, but he just wanted his son well, so he told me to do whatever I needed to. I walked over to the guy in the hospital bed and laid my hand on his stomach again, and said very calmly, "Tormenting spirit, I command you to leave now and never bother this man again, in Jesus' name." That was it, the whole prayer. Boom: the guy stopped moving around and drifted off into heavy sleep.

The next day, I received a call from the dad to tell me his son was doing incredibly well and that he wanted to meet me. As I walked into the hospital room, the son, looking like a completely new man, was sitting up in his bed. He was reading in the book of Psalms and he was happy. The guy looked at me and said, "I felt something leave me when you prayed for me yesterday. I slept for over twelve hours straight after you prayed for me. What happened?" So, I began to share the gospel of Jesus with him. I told him if he would allow Jesus to take up residence in his heart, he would never have to worry about this happening again.

One week after this happened, the man drove forty-five minutes to come by my house and tell me all that had happened since I spoke to him. His wife had been about to leave him before he went into the hospital because of alcoholism, among other issues. However, after the encounter at the hospital with Jesus, she talked with him one more time. As she talked to him, she told him he seemed like a completely different person. He was happy to report to me that his wife stayed with him and that he had been hanging out with Jesus over the past week.

His wife came with him to meet me. She was ecstatic to have a brand-new husband. She said his demeanor was different and the torment was gone. She gave glory to Jesus and thanks for a restored marriage.

"Jesus is So Cool!"

April, Cadance, and I were at the hospital a couple of weeks after these miracles took place for my wife's baby appointment. While we were in the waiting room, I noticed a lady with a brace on her wrist. I approached her, said hello, and proceeded to share testimonies of Jesus healing people. I asked, "Why do you have that brace on your wrist?"

The lady told me that she had hurt it picking up her son and that something had popped. She thought it was possibly broken and that maybe some of the pain was from carpal tunnel. Her wrist was swollen and hurting, and she was at the doctor to get her wrist checked. I asked her if she would take the brace off and let me pray for her wrist.

As she took the brace off, I asked her eight-year-old son to come over and help me pray. The young boy put his hands gently on his mother's wrist and he repeated after me saying, "God, thank you for my mother. In Jesus' name, pain – I command you to leave; and wrist – I command you be healed, in Jesus' name. Thanks, God."

As the young boy finished praying, his mother was already in tears and the presence of God began to touch her. She began to move her wrist around: all the pain was gone. She regained full movement in her wrist and was completely pain-free, praise Jesus. Her young son looked up at me and said, "Jesus is so cool. This is freaky to see my mom's wrist get healed like this. Yay, Jesus is so super cool!" I concurred with the young man, "Yes, Jesus is amazing, and you have Him in your heart. You can pray for people anywhere you are, and Jesus will heal through you, young man."

We were in a hallway with several people around, so I began telling everyone around us what God had just done. As I was sharing with others about the miracle we just witnessed, the mom declared, "Look! My wrists are the same size. Even the swelling is gone now. Wow!" Whether at the hospital, work, church, yard sale, or wherever, God is with us and He wants to touch the world around us with His amazing love.

With Jesus as Lord of your life, all things are possible. If we will only believe, Jesus will manifest His love through us to the world, leaving zero doubt about this fact: God is love, and He is always good, always.

Revival at a Yard Sale

A friend of mine called one Saturday morning and asked if I would go with him to pray for a coworker with pancreatic cancer. My buddy picked me up around 8:00 a.m. and we started off toward Cairo, Georgia. As we rode in his truck, I shared many testimonies declaring the goodness of God, and my friend was very eager to witness his first miracle. Upon arrival at his coworker's house, we discovered they were having a yard sale. People were completely unaware of what Jesus was about to do in their midst, mulling around the yard looking for bargains.

My friend introduced me to his coworker, Shawn, and I immediately began sharing testimonies with him. As I told testimony after testimony, people who were perusing the items for sale began to inch their way towards us. Out of the corner of my eye I noticed several people leaning on a clothes rack paying close attention to what I was saying. Their shopping ceased as their ears became tuned into the Gospel.

One of the guys sitting beside Shawn had a bulky knee brace on. I asked him if he would take the brace off and allow me to pray for his knee. He looked a bit uncomfortable, but he agreed. I asked the man's wife to come over and pray with us. After a brief prayer, I asked the guy to test out his knee. He gingerly got up and began to walk. Much to his surprise, his knee felt incredibly well. For the duration of our visit, he left the bulky knee brace over on the grass as he continued to walk around.

Next, we prayed for Shawn, who had the pancreatic cancer. As soon as I finished praying for him, one of the guys leaning on the clothes rack called me over. This guy was blown away by the testimonies he had overheard, and he begin telling me about a car wreck that he had been in two weeks earlier. His sciatic nerve was messed up and his back was in a world of pain. Also, his right knee was in severe pain, his right foot could barely bend, and he had lost feeling below the knee in his right leg. When I found out the guy's wife was there, I asked her to come over and pray with us. We commanded his sciatic nerve, knee, and foot to be healed in Jesus' name. We also asked God to restore the feeling in his leg.

While this was happening, the guy looked up at me and exclaimed, "I feel heat in my back!" I told him to test out his back. He began moving and twisting his back without any pain. He began to get emotional and his wife lost it as she began weeping.

Next, the man tried out his knee. All the pain was gone, and his knee was not making a popping sound as it had before when he would bend it. Then the guy began rolling his foot around. It completely loosened up, and he could bend his foot normally. In addition to all of this, feeling was restored in his leg. God completely healed this guy outdoors at a yard sale. The guy gave me a huge bear hug and then began calling people on the phone and telling them what God had just done for him.

Other people came over for prayer, and God touched them as well. Revival broke out at a yard sale. My friend who'd asked me to accompany him was on cloud nine as he witnessed the power of God breaking out and lives being radically touched. People were crying as the presence of God touched them, and the eyes of their hearts were opened to how good God is—all while shopping at a yard sale.

Miracles Point to Jesus

One night at work, I received a phone call requesting me to meet some people in Bainbridge, Georgia, at their home to pray for a terminally ill cancer patient. I had never met them, but they had heard about me from someone they knew. I agreed to head over after work that night and pray with the lady who had called. When I arrived at the house, close to eleven people were there, ready to hear me share Jesus with them and pray.

I was excited, so at 10:30 p.m. the Holy Spirit and I began to flow and move in this house. I told them a couple of testimonies and then I prayed with the lady who had cancer. As soon as I finished praying with her, I heard the Holy Spirit tell me to pray with another lady in the house. I went over to her and told her God had just spoken to me, and I needed to pray with her right then.

As I grabbed her hand, I began to say what I heard God saying in my heart and the woman began to tremble and weep. I was telling her what God thought of her and what He was about to do to restore her marriage. The woman got completely rocked by the power of God. In fact, she was a nonbeliever who had come to the house as a skeptic because she thought the things she had heard were false. The woman knew I did not even know her name nor that of anyone else in the house, yet I had told her exactly what God said about all that she was going through. The power of God literally shook her. She encountered God in a mighty way, and she gave her heart to Jesus. She said she could literally feel a heartbeat in her hand as I was holding her hand and praying over her. She was in awe of all she experienced.

In less than a week, her husband, who had left her, miraculously returned and began to attend church with her regularly. Several people in this home were healed of various things as well.

A week later, the same woman invited me to meet a friend who was visiting from New York. When I walked towards him to meet him, he instantly got goose bumps all over his arms. He said, "Man, this is so weird." He told me when the lady began telling him she wanted us to meet, he had instantly gotten goose bumps all over him then as well. Needless to say, this "sign" had his full attention.

I shared the gospel with him, and the young man in his twenties gave his heart to Jesus right there at this house.

It is our great privilege as children of God to partner with the Holy Spirit to bring Jesus His eternal reward. Jesus paid the highest price so we and everyone else could be restored to Father God. Miracles point to the goodness of God. When you hear of these and other testimonies, don't you give glory and praise to God? If you did not hear these testimonies because we were afraid to share them, or worse, we didn't believe God enough for them to manifest, then the praise and glory He receives from them would not be possible.

The body of Christ is to absolutely be filled with the Holy Spirit, and there are to be many miracles, signs, and wonders that all point to the goodness and glory of God. Jesus Himself said, "If I do not do the works of My Father, do not believe Me; but if I do, though you do not believe Me, believe the works, that you may know and believe that the Father is in Me, and I in Him" (John 10:37–38). The miracles pointed to the Father, because Jesus clearly stated, "Most assuredly, I say to you, the Son can do nothing of Himself, but what He sees the Father do; for whatever He does, the Son also does in like manner" (John 5:19). Also, in John 14:12 Jesus clearly states that whoever believes in Him will do the same works Jesus did—and even greater works, because Jesus was going to the Father.

Paul states in Romans 15:19 that the gospel of Jesus is only presented fully when power accompanies the Word: "They were convinced by the power of miraculous signs and wonders and by the power of God's Spirit. In this way, I have fully presented the Good News of Christ" (NLT). In like manner, if God is not confirming His Word that we preach with signs and miracles following—with fruit—then we can't expect people to listen to the gospel and repent (change the way they think). However, even if they don't believe what we say, God confirms with signs and wonders that what we preach is true.

A young married couple came to my wife and me one day asking for prayer. They had been trying unsuccessfully to get pregnant for almost three years and did not know what else to do. We prayed with them, and about two weeks later they came to see me to share the most exciting news: they were expecting their first child!

As I talked with them, I felt the Holy Spirit share with me that she was carrying a girl. I shared this with the mother and she began weeping tears of joy. She told me it has always been her dream since a young age to mother a girl. She even had the full name already picked out for her daughter. Now flash-forward to this present day: this couple has a beautiful, healthy six-month-old little girl. Our God is the Author of life.

I remember being at a Seminole County home football game a while back and getting a word of knowledge in the stands. I was visiting with a friend, talking about Jesus, and I felt the Holy Spirit tell me He wanted to heal someone's shoulders. I was surrounded by people and had no idea who it was. So, I said, "Holy Spirit, I really need to know exactly who it is because I don't want to just ask this whole group of random people to tell me whose shoulders are hurting." I was patient, trusting that He would show me who it was with pain in the shoulders. About two minutes later, He highlighted a lady to my right, and I knew it was her.

I told my friend I would be back in just a minute, and I slid down the row and got the lady's attention. I said, "Hey, you have bad shoulder pain, even right now, don't you?" She looked totally shocked and said yes, she did. She wondered how in the world I could possibly know her shoulders were hurting. I told her I knew because God just told me He wanted to heal her. Would she allow me to lay my hands on her shoulders and pray? She said sure, and in the middle of the football game I gently placed my hands on her shoulders and in Jesus' name commanded all the pain to leave. The lady felt a noticeable heat begin to move in her shoulders, and all the pain left.

A lady asked me one day to join her, her family friend, and her ten-year-old son for breakfast. This lady was so encouraged because she had witnessed several miracles with people that she personally knew. She was a Christian, but up until recently she had never witnessed the power of God being manifested like this. She wasn't even sure she believed the miracles of the Bible still happened today. However, after seeing it with her own eyes, she was now fully convinced that the miraculous was still very much an active part of Christianity.

I don't argue with Christians who don't believe miracles happen today. I've learned a much better way. I trust the Holy Spirit to show up and do what only He can do because I have faith. Once people encounter the power of God and are healed themselves, it is kind of hard for them to argue about it anymore. I'm not here to prove a point of view; I'm here to love you and let God's love and power flow without hindrance as He performs His Word.

The mother wanted me to meet them to share some more testimonies and give Bible verses about healing. At the end, her young son wanted prayer for an ingrown toenail. This young man has battled severe ingrown toenails in his big toe since his first year of life. He has had multiple surgeries to have it repaired. After the surgeries failed, the podiatrist cauterized the toenail down the sides and told the family that he would never again suffer with ingrown toenails. However, it became painfully ingrown again. The boy lifted his foot up and I laid hands on it right there in the restaurant.

Two years after prayer, this now-twelve-year-old young man informed me that he has not had one ingrown toenail since prayer. He even took off his shoe and sock to reveal a perfectly grown toenail with no sign of the cauterization.

We also hear of God blessing people's farmland. A few weeks ago, a family asked for prayer because they expected to lose many crops because of excessive rain. The place that purchases part of their produce had just rejected many of their crops. However, after prayer, this family received word that the purchasing company had changed their policy and none of their crop would be rejected. This family is giving much thanks to the Lord.

A first-time mom asked for prayer, as she was having a hard time producing milk and was about to have to begin to feed her newborn with a bottle and formula. Immediately during prayer, the milk started flowing and for the past two weeks she has produced more than enough to feed her child naturally.

At a recent Seminole County football game, I had a gentleman come up the stands to see me. He had some wonderful news to share with me. About two years prior, we had talked for a minute at another football game; he had had a pounding headache and was asking people for aspirin. I grabbed his hand and I told him that if he would let me pray for him, God would heal him right then and there. He told me to go ahead and pray.

Flash-forward to the recent game. This same man came up to me and asked, "Do you remember praying for me a couple of years back at a game?" I told him that I did indeed remember. He said that not only did God heal him of the headache when I prayed for him, but for the past two years he has not had another headache since. One encounter with the presence of God—and no more headaches.

Jesus said these words in John 13:34–35, "A new commandment I give to you, that you love one another; as I have loved you, that you also love one another. By this all will know that you are My disciples, if you have love for one another." The gospel of Jesus boils down to this: love. We are to receive Jesus' love for us and, in turn, give that love back to Him and those around us. If we will submit to Him, He will take our lives and fashion us into the image and likeness of Himself: God is love. Apart from Him we can do nothing of any eternal significance, but with Him we can do all things.

I was shopping at a store in Bainbridge recently. I prayed with several people and made myself available for the love and power of God to touch these precious people. They were all strangers to me, yet God knew each person. One of the people I approached was a younger lady in a motorized wheelchair. I asked her how she was doing, and she revealed to me that she had just lost a child. The doctors had performed a procedure to remove the child from her body. She also told me she has been battling massive depression. I knelt beside her and prayed with her, releasing the love and joy of Jesus.

A few days later, at our Tuesday night service, a lady who attends our service approached me and told me of her conversation with a friend of hers. She asked me if I remembered praying with a woman recently in a store who had lost a child. I told her I indeed remembered. She said that was her friend, and she'd told her about what had happened when I prayed for her. She encountered the presence of God right there in in the store. God healed her instantly of the depression and she had an amazing sense of peace. She said she had not cried another tear since we meet several days earlier. At her next doctor's visit, she even refused the antidepressants the doctor tried to give her. She told the doctor about how God healed her and how everything had changed. The doctor tried to get her to take the medicine with her just in case she began to have those feelings again, but the young lady still refused them.

The Lord Knows Our Hearts

I went to eat at a restaurant in Dothan. On the way there, I was speaking with the Lord. I asked Him if there was anything He wanted me to share from His heart with the servers there. I thought about a young man that had waited on us before, so I asked God about him. The Lord said, "He wants to start a business." I asked the Lord to be more specific, and He replied, "He produces music now as a side business and he would like to open a sound studio down the road." I thought, "Wow, that is specific." I knew nothing of this young man except he worked in the restaurant I was about to eat at.

After being seated, my server came over and took my drink order; unfortunately, he was not the young man for whom I had a word. Unperturbed, I called the young man over to my table. I asked him for his name, then I told him my name and asked him if he wanted to start his own business. He said, "Sure I do. It would be great to be my own boss. I actually have a side business right now." At this point, I asked him to not tell me what that business was. I said, "You promote and produce music right now. And it's your dream to open a music studio." His eyes got surprisingly big and he said, "Get out of here, man! Get out. How do you know that?"

I told him what the Lord had told me, and then I shared how God wanted to be known as a Father to this young man. I also shared how God sent Jesus for us and that was how I was able to have a relationship with God. I told the guy some more words I felt like God was showing me about his future music studio. The young man had tears in his eyes. Next, I asked him if I could pray with him briefly. He was happy for me to pray with him, and he was so encouraged about how deeply involved God the Father was in the details of his life.

Later, I finished eating my meal and was heading out the door. I felt a tap on my shoulder and saw the young man standing there, smiling from ear to ear. He told me, "You will never know what today has meant to me. Thanks so much for sharing that with me. This is one of the best days of my life."

Chapter 3: Family

My wife and children are also powerful witnesses in public for Jesus. April sees many of the same types of miracles that I do. She prays with lots of people in public and loves to display God's love. One day, we were in Dothan at a gas station. An employee came out of the store and began to collect the trash as we were pumping gas.

April began to talk with the young man, whom God revealed had pain in his lower back. April then asked the man if he had pain in his lower back. He looked surprised and asked her how she knew that. April told him God revealed it to her and if he would let her pray for him, God would heal his back.

I had a front row seat for this conversation and the awesomeness that would ensue, as I was pumping gas. The young guy reluctantly agreed for April to pray for him.

April prayed a brief, but believing, prayer commanding the pain to leave his back in Jesus' name. The young man began to tear up and said, "I can feel the Spirit." The man then began to move up and down, twisting his back and trying it out. He began to get super excited as he realized all the pain was gone and God had just completely healed his back. At this point I ran over to them because I always want to be where God is moving. The presence and the love of God were tangible during this time.

The young man began to tell April how he had been a Christian earlier in his life. Over time, he had let his love of Jesus grow cold. However, because of this encounter, the young man decided to renew his love for Jesus. He was so encouraged by God's love for him.

Another day at work, April bumped into a coworker who had pain in his neck area. This coworker's neck was in such pain that he could barely move it. April asked him if she could pray for him and he said yes. As April prayed, he felt heat in his neck and the pain left. The coworker was very perplexed that he could feel heat. He was amazed at the way his neck immediately loosened up and the pain left. He has not had any more problems with his neck, and it has been several weeks since God healed him.

A Child Will Lead Them

My oldest daughter, Cadance, loves to pray and tell people about Jesus in public as well. Once over the Thanksgiving holidays, she and I were at a restaurant and a Spanish-speaking family of ten people sat down beside us. Before we left, Cadance went over to their table and told them in Spanish, "*Jesus* (Hay-SOOS) *es rey*." Translated to English, it means, "Jesus is King." We blessed them in Jesus' name, and they all smiled and thanked us.

Many times, when my family and I go to a store, Cadance will walk off with me. We go up to different people and strike up a conversation about Jesus and how much He loves them. Cadance is very bold and will pray with me for the people we meet. Many of these people can feel the tangible presence of God as we pray with them. Many of them cry, smile, get healed, and just enjoy the love of God in action through Cadance and me.

My seven-year-old daughter, Gabby, also enjoys praying for people in public. One day after school, Gabby ran into the house to tell me she saw a man on the side of the road that she wanted us to go back and pray for. She insisted we load up in our car and go back to where she saw the man. I told her we would go, and sure enough, right where she led me was the man she wanted to pray for. We got out, and I told the guy what Jesus had done for me and asked him if Gabby and I could pray with him. I am so encouraged by the love my children have for God and for people.

Words of Knowledge

One of the people who I have been teaching about the kingdom of heaven recently attended the Bainbridge State College graduation. As she sat in the crowd, God revealed to her that he wanted to heal back pain. She began to scan the people around her asking God to show her who the person was. A minute later, God highlighted a woman sitting a few rows in front of her. She later approached the woman and introduced herself. She laid her hand on the woman's back in the exact area that God had revealed the back pain was occurring. She asked if the woman was having back pain in this area, and the women answered yes. My friend prayed for the woman and instantly the pain ceased.

A few weeks later, April went to the dentist to have her teeth cleaned. As my wife and the dental hygienist talked, my wife was sharing testimonies about Jesus and His goodness. The hygienist then wanted to share something that happened to her mom at the most recent Bainbridge State College graduation. She said her mom was approached by a total stranger. The stranger told her mom that God revealed she had back pain and that He wanted to heal her. The hygienist told my wife that for the past month her mom has been completely pain-free. My wife told her what the stranger's name was and the hygienist said that was correct. How cool to see the kingdom of God growing in our area.

Jesus is alive, and He is the God who heals and forgives us (Psalm 103:3). On a typical Sunday morning service, the Holy Spirit gave April a word of knowledge. She said there were people who had severe neck pain that was causing bad headaches. Two people responded to this word and were both instantly healed after prayer. The next week at church, I approached these two individuals separately and asked them how the past week had been. The man told me he had been completely pain-free and he had full range of motion in his neck all week.

Next, I went over and spoke with the lady from the week before. She also told me that she had not had any more pain in her neck area and she had not had any headaches all week. A few weeks before we prayed with her, she had visited the doctor because of all the discomfort, pain, and headaches she was having. After examining her, the doctor had told her they thought it was an issue with a muscle in her neck and there wasn't much they could do for her. However, God is the great Healer and He took care of it in an instant. Thank God, He is always good, faithful, and full of love.

I love April's heart attitude toward God. She has a unique, genuine relationship with God built around love and complete trust. She is fully convinced that He is in constant communion with her. Recently we went on a date without our kids. As we were having lunch, we saw two ladies get seated in the booth behind us. April had seen these same two ladies about twenty minutes earlier in the mall. She realized that God wanted her to go up to these ladies and share His love with them.

She asked God what He wanted her to say to them. He responded that one of the ladies had a car that needed repair. April went over to the ladies, greeted them briefly, and asked which of them was having car trouble. One of the ladies responded that her car was absolutely broken down and in need of repair. April released God's heart for provision to have the car repaired and prayed with the ladies.

After this, April asked God for a word for our server at the restaurant. God indicated that the man was short on finances for a business he wanted to start. Sure enough, the young man was looking to start a landscaping business with his brother, and they lacked the finances to start it. After April shared that God was bringing the finances to supply the startup of their business, we prayed with the young man and encouraged him that God was indeed with him and that his business would be successful. We could tell the young man was very encouraged by this encounter with the presence of God.

After lunch, we went to a store to purchase some items. Before we got there, April had asked God for a name of a person she would minister to. She heard the name "Cindy." While I was in line at the register, my wife briefly left to go and get another item that was not in our cart. Upon reaching the employee, I looked at her name tag. Sure enough, it read Cindy.

So, I told my wife to get back in the line that I had just left because the girl that God told her she would meet was standing right there. As April waited to meet the lady, she asked God what He wanted to do for Cindy. God told April that Cindy had a problem with the arches in her feet. April began to tell Cindy what God had revealed to her. Cindy said she indeed had pain and problems with the arches of her feet. The presence and love of God was so amazing that the cashier next to Cindy stopped ringing up the person she was waiting on and stared in amazement at what was happening next to her.

I'm thankful for Christians like my wife, April, who are willing to hear the Father's heart for individuals and that April has the courage to step out in faith and bless those around her.

Love Never Fails

The Lord states in the New Living Translation, Jeremiah 22:16, "'He gave justice and help to the poor and needy, and everything went well for him. Isn't that what it means to know Me?' says the Lord." Wow—the Lord says that giving help to poor and needy people is a reflection of knowing the Lord. We are told to be imitators of God (Ephesians 5:1). God is love (1 John 4:8); that means we are to become love. We are to know our Father and allow Him to fashion us into pure love. Love is patient and kind (1 Corinthians 13:4). Love keeps no record of wrongs. Love is not self-seeking. Love never fails.

I know a lady who owned only one coat. She was in Atlanta, and it was freezing cold. As she was walking, she passed by a homeless lady with a child. This lady did not hesitate to walk over to the woman, take off her only coat, and drape it around the homeless mother and her baby. She told her how much God loves her and walked away. Love never fails.

I know a man who was getting breakfast in my hometown. He spotted a couple with a sign stating they were homeless and trying to get to West Virginia. The man heard the Holy Spirit instruct him to give $220 to the strangers. He did not hesitate; he went straight to the ATM and withdrew the funds. He came back, got out of his car, and told the couple how much God loved them. He then gave them the money, prayed with them, and watched the love of God fill their hearts. Love never fails.

I know a man who once was eating at a restaurant in Colquitt, Georgia. He heard the Holy Spirit tell him to go and get $300 for the three waitresses working in his seating area. He did not hesitate. He got the money and called the three ladies over to him, giving each one hundred dollars. He prayed with them and watched as all three ladies experienced the radical presence of the loving Father descend upon them. Love never fails.

I know a man who was shopping for Christmas gifts for his own children. He had sixty dollars in cash to buy them gifts. While shopping, he saw a lady buying her kids a few items for Christmas. She was in rags and he heard the Holy Spirit tell him to walk over and give the sixty dollars to her. As he was being obedient, he watched as the love of God invaded and lives were wrecked by the presence of a loving Father. Love never fails.

I know an individual who gave their entire week's pay to a family in need because he heard the Holy Spirit tell him to give, even though the individual certainly needed it himself. The love of God flowed in like a flood and the family saw the goodness of God. Love never fails.

God Himself is a giver. God so loved the world that He gave (John 3:16). He gave the greatest gift ever known to all of creation.

He gave Himself through His one and only Son, Christ Jesus. On the cross He was naked, unrecognizable, tortured, bleeding, cramping, hungry, thirsty, dying in agony. Hanging there for you. Hanging there for me. God is love. Righteous people are poised to show radical generosity just like their Father in Heaven. Dare to be radically generous because you have been transformed into love.

God's Compassionate Heart

In a recent meeting, an older lady complained about her shoulder really bothering her. She could not lift it over her head and it had been bothering her for quite some time. Cadance prayed over her shoulder and instantly the pain left—she could raise her arm all the way above her head. I love the fact that children get the same Holy Spirit that adults do, and God loves to move through children and adults. We are all His kids.

I attended my sister-in-law's wedding in Saint Simons, Georgia. It was beautiful, and I watched the Lord touch so many lives while we were there. At the wedding rehearsal, I met my sister-in-law's father. He had been in a terrible accident and his body was severely damaged. He had mostly recovered at that point; however, his wrist was still in terrible pain and he had been rehabbing it. After talking to him briefly, I asked him to let me hold his wrist. I prayed and then walked away to take my seat with my children. Two weeks later, my sister-in-law told April that from the moment I prayed for her father's wrist, all the pain left and his mobility was completely restored.

After the wedding, we attended a reception with lots of different people. A man we did not know came and sat at the table with my family. We talked briefly, and then I asked the Holy Spirit if anything was bothering this guy. The Holy Spirit told me, "He has heart issues." I moved out of my chair and sat right next to the man. I asked him what was going on with his heart. The man looked at me stunned and said, "It is incredible that you know that. I have a blocked heart valve and I'm scheduled to go in to see what type of surgery will be done on my heart." I shared the love of God with this man and then told him that if he would allow me to pray with him, God would heal his heart and he would not need surgery. I prayed, and the man was aware of God's presence and love. I believe that God absolutely healed his heart in these moments. This man was not a Christian. However, all of this opened the door for me to share Christ with him.

After the wedding, April took Cadance to a school event in Perry, Georgia. As April stood by one of our bus drivers, the Holy Spirit told her that the lady beside her was having severe problems with her right arm. April asked her if she had pain shooting from her shoulder and down to her arm. The bus driver was surprised and told my wife that she had indeed been having terrible pain in her right arm for some time. She had seen the chiropractor multiple times about this issue. April asked if she could pray for her because she believed God was about to heal her. She prayed for the lady and went back to watching our daughter perform. About a week later, my wife saw the bus driver again and the lady told my wife that all the pain had completely left, and she had felt amazing since April prayed for her.

At one of our favorite Japanese restaurants, April and I were sitting at the sushi bar eating our supper. The Holy Spirit spoke to April, revealing to her that the guy serving us had neck pain. She asked our server, Jack, if his neck was bothering him. He looked surprised as he confirmed that his neck has been bothering him for some time now, along with his back. April told Jack that Jesus loved him very much and then asked him if she could briefly pray for him. He consented and after a brief prayer, he began to move his neck around. As he moved it from side to side, all the pain was instantly gone. Also, his back was completely healed, and he smiled so big as he discovered that God had instantly healed him right there at the sushi bar.

One typical school workday, one of April's coworkers approached her with a desperate plea. She was pregnant and had just received news from the doctors that her baby would most likely be born with Down syndrome. This lady immediately came to someone she knew could touch the heart of God through relationship. My wife shared the Father's heart with this precious lady, then prayed with her. After prayer, April told the lady that when she was tested again she would receive a different report. April told her she would learn that her baby was completely healthy.

One week later, the coworker came excitedly to April's classroom with outstanding news. The doctors had run more tests. The results were in: her baby was completely healthy, and they could find no evidence whatsoever that her baby would have Down syndrome.

On one of our first far-away ministry trips together, April and I traveled to Milwaukee, Wisconsin, and to Chicago, Illinois, to share the gospel. The first night, many people encountered the presence of the Holy Spirit. Twelve out of fourteen people who received prayer were healed the first night. One boy, eleven years old, had worn glasses since he was five. He received prayer for his eyesight, and Jesus healed him instantly. He began reading signs all over the sanctuary that he could not have read without his glasses. The young boy stood before the congregation with his mother and began to weep tears of joy as Jesus totally restored his eyesight. An hour later I spoke with him, and he told me he had worn glasses for six years and now he would no longer need his glasses. He was so full of joy and praise for our Lord Jesus.

Another man in his forties had been in a work accident that severely injured his back six years earlier. He had multiple surgeries, yet his back was still in constant pain. He received prayer and began to move his back around. To his delight and exuberance, all the pain left instantly, and God healed his back completely. All the people celebrated the goodness of God together as their family members and fellow church members shared testimonies of God healing them. Many other people received healing in these meetings and many people received encouraging words from the Lord. Others were set free of addictions and other torments.

Walking in Favor

I love the favor of the Lord. April and I recently experienced the favor of the Lord on our return flight home from our ministry trip in Milwaukee and Chicago. As we were getting on the flight, I noticed the lady checking our boarding passes was pregnant. After saying hello, I asked her if I could do something awesome for her. The airline employee, Kim, said, "Sure." I took her hand and begin to pray for the presence, favor, blessing, and glory of the Lord to be released upon her. After this brief prayer, she was tearing up as the presence of the Lord was heavy upon her.

Another airline employee beside her said to me in astonishment, "Hey, I have chill bumps all over me right now. What is happening to us?" I told both women that it was the glory of the Lord and they were experiencing the Holy Spirit. They were amazed at the glory they were feeling, and we told them farewell.

When my wife and I boarded the plane, we discovered we were seated in the very last row. We were tired from a long weekend of serving others, and as we settled in for the long trip home we noticed the pregnant flight employee, Kim, approaching us. She said to us, "Excuse me, but can you and your wife grab your things and come this way with me, please?" We said sure, and as we followed her she stated that there was no way she was letting us sit at the back of the plane. She escorted us to first class.

As our plane got on the runway, we were directed back to the airport for a new flight path and to refuel because of bad weather. We were delayed an hour from our original departure time, and most people on our plane had either missed or were in danger of missing their connecting flight this late at night. As we landed, April and I had only ten minutes to make our connecting flight in Charlotte with no more flights out that night. If we had been in the last seats on the plane, we would have certainly missed our flight. However, we were the first people off the plane and we ran through the airport to our next flight to take us to Tallahassee. We arrived at the gate to find the door was closed and had already been locked, but the lady saw us and unlocked it and let us go to the plane. We were the last ones to board, and we boarded with two minutes to spare. Thanks for the favor of the Lord. If not for His goodness, we would have missed our flight and been stuck overnight in Charlotte instead of arriving home to see our three precious children.

Chapter 4: Olive Theater

"You are a Fraud"

I n April of 2013, as I transitioned from managing the restaurant into full-time ministry, I began to hold meetings on Tuesday nights at the Olive Theatre in my hometown. This theater was used by the community to do all sorts of plays and to host other events. We saw many different miracles of God's power in this place. On the first night I held a meeting, the first lady through the doors greeted me by saying, "I have heard about these miracles, but I don't believe in any of this. I came to satisfy my curiosity that you are a fraud and that God does not do these things you say." I was taken aback, but I gave her a hug and told her I was glad she came.

Toward the end of the meeting that night, the presence of God was glorious, and several people had already been healed. The "skeptical lady" had brought along a friend who was about thirty-five years old and had been injured eight years earlier while riding a roller coaster at a theme park. Her neck hurt much of the time. She had been on pain medication since the accident and often visited chiropractors. I prayed for her, but nothing happened. Her neck was still in bad shape.

The "skeptical lady" smirked a bit when nothing changed in her friend's neck. I heard the Holy Spirit instruct me to have the "skeptical lady" lay hands on her friend's neck. She was reluctant at first, but I told her we had nothing to lose. Either she would be proven right in her own eyes, or her friend would leave the building healed. It was a real "win-win" situation.

She laid her hand on her friend's neck, and I told her what to say. "Jesus, in Your name I command this injury to leave, and I thank you for healing this neck. Amen." To her and my amazement, the friend receiving prayer began to weep uncontrollably as the presence of God rested upon her. Her neck loosened immediately and all the pain from the past eight years vanished as Jesus healed her completely. These two women became regulars in my meetings, and they told of God's power to heal. My "skeptical" new friend became a believer in Jesus and developed a relationship with Him. Her husband would also later get saved and be radically delivered by the Lord Jesus.

Hungry for His Goodness

In our second meeting, several more people were healed. However, as the meeting concluded, I noticed a lady with a wrist brace on. I approached her and asked if she had received prayer and why she wore the brace. She had not been prayed for and she wore the brace because of severe carpal tunnel syndrome; she said it was a part of her life and that she had just learned to manage the pain the best she could. I asked her to remove the brace and asked her daughter to lay hands on her mother's wrist. Neither of these ladies had ever witnessed a miracle and we were just meeting for the first time.

As we laid hands on the mom, the presence of the Holy Spirit rested on her, and she began to laugh and cry simultaneously. All the pain left and she has not had any issue with carpal tunnel pain since. God is so very good. From this miracle, the daughter, who was in her mid-thirties, had her heart set ablaze for the Lord. She has had a huge change in her life and has been speaking in jails and teaching at various other places.

A lady heard about the miracles and the outpouring of the Holy Spirit we had been experiencing at the Olive Theatre, and she drove over two hours to attend a Tuesday night meeting. After the meeting, she was blown away at what she had seen and experienced, and she asked for my phone number. A couple of days later, she called me and asked if she could drive to Donalsonville again to meet with me one-on-one and if I would share more testimonies with her. Of course, I was thrilled to meet with her and share over three hours' worth of testimonies of the miracles, signs, wonders, and salvations that I have witnessed. She told us how in her city they had been teaching on healing for years, and yet they hadn't seen people healed. This lady was hungry enough to see the power of God to drive from over two hours away to be where God was pouring out His Spirit.

As I shared testimonies with her, the Holy Spirit gave me a word of knowledge. He told me that she was having severe knee pain and that He wanted to heal her. I said to her in the middle of one of the testimonies, "You have bad knee pain, don't you?" She started grinning and said that for a long time she has battled sore knees that have kept her from working out and playing sports because of the pain. I called my wife and kids over, and we commanded her knees to be healed in Jesus' name. The lady began to move her knees, and she even squatted all the way to the floor without pain. This was the first time in years that she had been able to squat without severe pain, praise God. Before she left, I explained to her how I was going to lay hands on her and pray with her, and she would begin to see the miraculous break out in her city. A couple of days later, I received a message from her that she prayed with a lady who had a growth on her stomach and that the growth had fallen off in the woman's hands.

I was invited by this new friend to help at a food drop in her hometown of Quitman, Georgia. So, I drove over and began talking with lots of different people who needed food. While their physical hunger had brought them, many of them were about to be fed spiritual food. I prayed with many people and watched the power and love of God touch many people. One elderly lady was with her family, and I asked if any of them needed prayer. They said no thanks, but the grandma said, "Yes, my back and neck have been bothering me for a long time."

So, I prayed for her back and instantly it was healed. After a couple of times of praying for her neck with another friend helping, we saw breakthrough in this area as well. The grandma was beaming with the biggest smile as she moved around pain-free.

Next thing I knew, the family members who had said no to prayer were lining up for prayer. Later, I approached another lady that was helping with the food drop and asked her what she needed God to do. She told me her back was in constant pain from degenerating discs. I prayed for her and then told her to test it out. She said, "I can't bend over." I told her to try and see. Next thing we saw, the lady was touching her toes, pain-free, and twisting her body from side to side like a wide-eyed child. She exclaimed, "There isn't any pain. I'm going to go home and get to all the work that I haven't been able to do." She was smiling from ear to ear and laughing at her newfound freedom.

After the food drop, my friend took me to a different church to meet a pastor friend of hers. As we walked in, we discovered that they were having a leadership meeting and certainly not expecting us. I instantly introduced myself to the pastor and asked if anyone there needed prayer. I also shared a testimony or two. One woman could not lift her shoulders over her head without severe pain. We prayed for her three times, and on the third time she was completely healed. The lady beside her got healed of shoulder pain as well—and no one prayed for her. Also, while I was sharing a testimony with them and praying for a lady with carpal tunnel syndrome, the Holy Spirit again healed another woman's knee, even though no one prayed for her. How truly incredible to see the glory of God showing up at each place I went.

A couple of weeks later at my local church I told the testimony about my trip to Quitman. As I was recounting the events of that amazing trip, God showed up and did it again. A woman in attendance was completely healed of shoulder pain without anyone praying for her. The lady told me that while I shared the testimony, she began to experience a weightiness resting upon her shoulders. After that, her shoulders felt at ease and for the next couple of weeks she was able to work at home using her shoulders, which were completely pain-free. No one prayed for her and no one except her knew that God was healing her. She simply sat and listened to me as I told about God's goodness and His healing of the other ladies in Quitman. The word "testimony" in the Bible literally means "to do again." As I gave the "testimony" to the church, God showed up and did it again.

One day, before I was to speak at the Olive Theatre, I was hanging out with God. I asked Him if there was anything specific He wanted to do in the next meeting. As I closed my eyes and quieted my heart, I saw a picture of a hand with severe arthritis. I knew God wanted to heal a person's hand.

So, in the meeting the next night, I called out the word of knowledge that God was going to heal arthritis in the hand. Sure enough, a couple of minutes later, I heard a commotion as people in one section began wildly praising God because He had just completely healed a woman with severe arthritis in the hand. I walked over to her, and she was smiling, laughing, crying, and shocked all at the same time. You see, the arthritis in her hand was so bad, she could not even come close to making a fist. However, after I called out the word, she received prayer from some believers and she began to be able to completely open and close her hand pain-free. She continued repeatedly making a fist as we all gave glory and honor to God.

The next week, she came to the meeting and said she had been cracking pecans all day because her hand was still pain-free and she was still making a fist without any hindrance. Also in this meeting, I called out a word for back pain. Several people stood up in the middle of my preaching and received prayer, and five out of six people were instantly healed.

Later in the week, I was at another meeting and before I got there, God revealed to me that someone was going to be there who was experiencing pain in their left hand that went up into the arm. Before the pastor began to speak, I relayed this information to him and we asked if anyone was specifically having this problem. Immediately, a woman raised her hand, and we went over to pray with her. God healed her, and after the meeting she came over and gave me the biggest hug while showing me how she was moving her left arm, hand, and shoulder without any pain. She told me she had been to the doctor and he'd told her that if it was not better within a week she would probably require surgery. However, God touched her, and now she was pain-free and surgery-free.

A teenage girl and her mom attended a meeting a while back for the first time. The girl came in eager expectation for God to touch her because she had heard about some of the miracles we were witnessing. We began to pray for the sick at the end of the meeting and the young girl received prayer. For the past five years she had had a terrible condition in her stomach. Her stomach would shrink and expand at dangerous intervals and only six percent of her stomach lining functioned properly at times. She was forced to eat a strict diet on a regular schedule of six meals a day or risk getting very sick. In addition to this, she took medication daily for her stomach.

Two weeks after getting prayer, the teenage girl attended the meeting again. She shared her incredible testimony of God's mercy with me at the end of the meeting. For the past two weeks, she had not taken any medication. On top of that, she had been eating whenever she felt hungry. She would much rather eat like that, as opposed to eating six meals a day at predetermined times. Just for good measure, she had been rigorously working outside in the South Georgia heat without complications as well.

Chapter 5: Church Testimonies

I was on my way with my wife to speak at a Celebrate Recovery meeting in Southwest Georgia. I had just begun to learn about words of knowledge and what they were. On the drive there, I got my first word of knowledge. God revealed to me that He was going to heal back pain. When we arrived at the meeting, the only person there that I had ever met before was the pastor of the church. After saying hello to him, I greeted some of the people gathered there. I also shook the hand of a healthy-looking man who appeared to be in his early forties. As I shook his hand, God revealed to me that he was the one with back pain. In addition to this, God let me know exactly where the pain was: in his lower back.

As we moved toward the sanctuary and away from the fellowship hall, I went up to the man and put my hand on the lower left-hand side of his back and said, "You have bad pain right here, don't you?" His eyes grew wide and he said yes. He also told me he couldn't sleep at night and that he was taking powerful prescription pills for the pain. I told him that God was about to heal him. After praying for him, all the pain left immediately, and I received a report later in the week that he had been sleeping at night. After God healed this man, I told the people there that since God had healed that man's back, if there were any other people with back pain they should come forward.

Another lady with the same issues came forward, and God healed her too. After this, I preached the gospel and asked if any of these people in this alcohol program didn't know Jesus. Three people came forward weeping, and all of them accepted Jesus to be Lord of their life. Many others came forward for prayer as the power of God swept through the place. The pastor was amazed at what God accomplished that night. He told me it was the most unique, fruitful Celebrate Recovery meeting he had ever witnessed.

I was invited to speak in a local church in my hometown. After preaching, I wanted us to begin to pray for the sick. April had a word of knowledge from the Lord right before we began ministering to the sick. The Lord revealed to her that someone in the building had numbness in their right foot and leg. She called out that word, and a lady was there with numbness in her right foot and leg. We prayed for this lady and God healed her. Her daughter told us a couple of days later that her mom was completely pain-free in her right foot and leg. She was able to walk and get around much better than in the past.

In addition to this miracle, a young boy was brought to us for prayer. His mom told us he was a fourth grader and that for three years he had suffered terrible pain in his stomach. The family had taken him to numerous doctors and specialists over the past three years, and none of the doctors could figure out the cause of the boy's problems or identify his condition. Anytime the boy had any milk or dairy products, he got violently sick and had terrible stomach pains. This also happened with various other foods that were introduced into his diet.

The mom brought him up to us and the power of God touched him. The boy told his mom that when we laid hands on his stomach, he felt heat go through it. The boy believed Jesus had healed him right then and there. So, that night when they got home, he wanted a big glass of milk. In the past, having a glass of milk would make him terribly sick; however, this was not a usual day, because the boy had just had an incredible encounter with Jesus. He drank the glass of milk and there was no pain or any other symptoms. Not only that, but he began to drink milk at school and remained completely pain-free. April talked to the little boy just the other day and said he was smiling and so excited that he could now eat and drink things without any pain and sickness. It has been over four years since this incredible miracle. The boy has been pain-free and eating as he pleases.

The House Church

Several years ago, I was invited by a friend to speak at a house church. Aside from the guy who invited me to speak, I had never met any of the people and I knew nothing about them. As I was giving testimonies and preaching, the fire of God was burning inside of me. Most of the people at this meeting were over thirty. However, there was one girl there who was only twelve years old. In the middle of my preaching, I pointed to her and began to prophesy over her. I told her that God had not called her to live like the other kids at her school because she was to be set apart to Him. I told her God was about to use her right away to do the impossible. I spoke to her for about three minutes as if no one else was in the room.

The young girl began crying profusely and trembling. As I was speaking to her, she raised her hand. I asked her to speak. She told us that while I was preaching, she prayed. She asked God that if I were telling the truth and God still healed people today, would God heal her little two-year-old sister. She asked God to have me call her out if He would heal her sister. She said as soon as she prayed this, I called her out for three straight minutes, speaking only to her, and told her that God was about to use her now to do the impossible.

I asked her what was wrong with her little sister. She told me that her little sister had fallen into a bonfire two days earlier and that paramedics had rushed her to the nearest burn victims' unit. The doctors told the family that she would be in the hospital a minimum of four weeks and she would require extensive skin grafts to try to repair her skin. The doctors said the inside of her palms would be scarred and there wasn't anything they could do about that. Also, the little girl couldn't eat, and the doctors were about to put in a feeding tube.

So we prayed with the twelve-year-old, Shirley. I told her to get her parents to take her the next day to the hospital and that God would heal her little sister, Melissa. Shirley wanted me to go because she thought God would only heal people through me, but I told her I had nothing to do with it. Jesus is the healer and He was with Shirley, so I told her Jesus was all she needed.

The next day on Tuesday, Shirley's mom took her out of school to send her to the burn victim's unit. When Shirley got to her sister's hospital room, she climbed into bed with Melissa and began to pray for her. The doctors tried to feed Melissa one more time before putting in the feeding tube, and Melissa began to eat immediately when Shirley began to pray! So, the doctors didn't have to put the tube in.

Over the next two days, the doctors watched as Melissa's skin began to heal and grow from the outside in. Melissa's skin was completely healed over the next two days—even the inside of her palms were completely healed. Melissa doesn't have any scars at all! The doctors were stunned, and they never did any skin grafts. Melissa got to go home after only eight days in the hospital instead of the minimum twenty-eight days the doctors told them it would be. Jesus completely healed Melissa's skin. The family even sent me before and after pictures: truly incredible!

From this one miracle, several of Shirley's family members gave their hearts to Jesus, including Shirley's mother. The whole family saw the power of Jesus and believed in Him. "For the kingdom of God is not in word but in power" (1 Corinthians 4:20). God used Shirley, a twelve-year-old girl, to display His power, glory, and mercy by healing Melissa's skin for all to see. Salvations came from this miracle, and Shirley has since been praying in public for strangers and seeing more miracles happen.

God wants all His children to display His kingdom in power and love everywhere we go. If you will only believe, you will see the glory of God in your own life (John 11:40). We were made for His glory (Isaiah 43:7), in the image of God (Genesis 1:27), to destroy the works of the devil (1 John 3:8). In everyday life, we can see Jesus heal, restore, and set people free through us, our lives surrendered to Him.

Healed of Cancer

I was invited to speak in a local Baptist church. The power of God was there, and I called for the sick to come forward for prayer. Bobby came down and told me he had colon cancer. He had been receiving treatment for the cancer for about three months without really seeing any improvement. The doctors would check him every Monday. So, on this Sunday we prayed, and the power of God touched Bobby.

The following day at the restaurant, a tall, elderly man and his wife came in. They were both in tears and smiles. They came straight up to me saying, "Thank you, and praise God." I had no idea who they were, but they grabbed me and hugged me. After a moment, I asked who they were. They informed me that they were Bobby's parents and he had just found out some wonderful news—the doctors had just done another check for cancer in his body, and they could not find any trace.

Bobby has since been back over the past year for checkups, and he is still completely cancer-free. So, for three months no improvement, and then one touch from Jesus and all the cancer was gone and has stayed gone. Philippians 2:9 states that Jesus is the name above every other name. Jesus' name is so much higher than cancer or any other disease or disability. Jesus has even defeated death (Hebrews 2:14).

The Fire of God

In this same service, another man came down for prayer. John had been suffering from terrible stomach pains for weeks; he was losing weight and was very weak. The doctors couldn't figure out what was causing the sickness. We prayed for John in this service and the power of God touched him as well. The pains in his stomach ended, his strength returned, and the next day he was able to work at his job without any complications. Also, John's heart was set on fire by the power of the gospel. He began to tell people all over the place about Jesus healing his body. John also began to pray for people in public. His life was changed by an awesome encounter with Jesus.

I had the opportunity to preach at a small church in Miller County. The presence of God was amazing, and we really had a great time that service. April got a word of knowledge from the Holy Spirit that someone present was experiencing a sharp, needlelike pain down the left side of their body above the hip. Sure enough, a lady there fit the description and when we prayed for her, God healed her pain instantly. One lady at this meeting encountered the love of God while we prayed for her in such an amazing way. She was so moved by what she experienced that at the end of the service, she wanted to sing a song of worship to God. She sang without instruments and without ever having sang in church like this, but it was amazing because real worship flowed from her heart. It is always so fun for me to see people experience God and watch how lives are changed in one real encounter with Him.

I was invited to speak at a youth bonfire in Bainbridge, Georgia. April, Cadance, and I showed up at the bonfire ready to see Jesus blow the socks off these kids. Kids from all different church denominations and backgrounds were there. I shared my testimony with them and then I began to share some testimonies of different miracles I had seen. The presence of God was very real as I spoke.

I pointed at one young lady and I told her that the fire of God was about to fill her up. She began to cry profusely and tremble as the power of God began to shake her. This went on for thirty or forty minutes as I continued to preach. I then called out a word of knowledge for someone there with terrible pain in their left shoulder. Sure enough, the mom whose land we were on had been having chronic pain in her left shoulder. When I placed my hand on her shoulder, she felt heat begin to move around her shoulder and all the pain left immediately.

I also had a word of knowledge that someone had a messed-up left leg from some type of accident. A tall kid limped up on crutches and said he had just had surgery on his left leg from a car accident. We prayed for his leg and he felt heat in it as well. He put down the crutches and began to test out his leg. All the pain was completely gone and he was walking normally. The forty or so teenagers at this bonfire were excited about what they witnessed God do firsthand for their friends and loved ones.

After this, April had a word of knowledge for a left ankle that was hurting and another word for someone with pain in the lower left side of their back. I called out these two words of knowledge and asked who they were for. A young boy and a young lady came up for prayer. The boy had injured his left ankle at tennis practice earlier in the week; he had a terrible sprain and was limping badly. We prayed for him and then had him test out the ankle. He felt heat in his ankle and began to jog around us without any pain. The young lady who came up for the word with pain in the lower left side of her back had recently had surgery there and had lingering pain in that area. As we prayed for her, she began to cry and she felt the fire of God begin to touch her back. All the pain left, and she was completely blown away at God's love for her and that He would heal her in an instant like that.

On this night we saw no fewer than four people healed; we also saw the fire of God fall as many of the teens wept under the power of God. It took us over thirty minutes to leave after the meeting was over because we had so many teenagers wanting to come up and tell my wife and me what God had done for them. Many of the teens had felt heat and a level of the presence of God like never before. I saw the hunger in these kids to know their heavenly Father increase in incredible measure in just one awesome encounter with the Holy Spirit.

It is my prayer that young people all over the world will encounter the real, tangible presence of the Holy Spirit. Religious activity and men's traditions keep young people from experiencing their Father in a real, amazing way. If our young people can be allowed to experience the Holy Spirit, they will not want to turn to the things of this world for fulfillment. They will find their identity as a son or daughter of the living God, Yahweh.

I was in the most amazing Easter service one morning at my home church. The power of God broke out during the service. People were healed, and different people had their hearts set ablaze by the Holy Spirit. One of the people healed that day was having constant pain in her neck. This lady had had an accident riding a horse over twenty years earlier, which had caused the lingering neck pain. Well, one touch from Jesus is enough; and after she'd experienced twenty years of pain, Jesus healed her neck completely. She told us that her neck had been throbbing even during the beginning of church, but when we prayed for her, God completely healed her neck and all the pain was gone.

Power of the Prophetic

I have also been a part of watching the prophetic flow in this walk with God. I was in a Sunday morning service in Donalsonville where I had been invited to speak. I was only familiar with a handful of people in the meeting. After preaching, I roamed through the congregation praying with different individuals and came to a young man I had never met before. As I began to pray for him, the Lord spoke to me about his life. I began to say what I heard God saying in my heart. The man was blown away at the accuracy with which I spoke. He knew there was no way I could possibly know all the things I was saying to him without it being from God.

I told him that his dream was to rap and that I could see him writing many songs. Recently, this young man had given his heart to Jesus. The dream of his heart was then put on hold because he thought God would not be OK with him doing what he wanted to do. However, I told him God had placed that desire in his heart and that he would continue to write songs—only, these songs would glorify and exalt Jesus. I told him he would lead a generation in worship through rapping and that many people would worship Jesus to different music other than the traditional stuff he was familiar with. The young man was blown away. He chased me down after the meeting to tell me that everything I had said to him was completely accurate and that he had been confused about what to do with the music dream in his heart. Ever since he was a young boy, he told me, he had been writing songs. God brought clarity to his heart and propelled him toward the destiny God was calling him to.

1 Corinthians 14:1 tells us, "Pursue love, and desire spiritual gifts, but especially that you may prophesy." 1 Corinthians 14:3 continues, "But he who prophesies speaks edification and exhortation and comfort to men." We see how prophecy is such a huge part of the Holy Spirit speaking through yielded believers to strengthen, encourage, and comfort the body of Christ.

Three years later, we were holding a youth event at my local church. Several guys were leading the youth in worship, including Christian rappers. There was one young guy who was so incredibly talented and anointed while rapping as the youth worshipped God. I bumped into him after the service and told him how awesome he did. Later, April asked me if I had realized who the amazing young worship leader was. I had not recognized him because he had cut all his hair off since I had prophesied over him three years earlier. In addition, I had lost a lot of weight and shaved my head so the young guy did not recognize me, either. A couple of days later, he attended our church again and we rejoiced to finally see each other. I got to watch him worship and lead youth into the presence of God through songs he had written and performed within my local church. How amazing to watch a prophetic word come to pass before your very eyes!

One Sunday morning at church, a lady came up to me and asked me to pray for her husband. He was having severe hip pain that had been going on for almost three months. So, I went over and prayed for him and nothing happened; he was still in terrible pain. About a minute later, I felt the Holy Spirit instruct me to go back over to him and just lay my hand on his shoulder, not even speaking a word.

Just a few seconds later, the pastor called the guy I had just prayed for up to give the announcements for the week. As he started to walk toward the front, he began to get blasted by the Holy Spirit! He began weeping, and as he got to the front of the church he could not even compose himself to give the announcements. Instead, he started praising God because the severe pain in his hip was completely gone. Through tears of joy, he tried to share what had just happened. Due to the raw power of God he experienced, he even forgot part of the announcements he was supposed to make and later in the service had to go back to the front a second time to give the rest of the announcements.

After three months of excruciating hip pain, God had healed him in a moment's time. Subsequently, the pastor asked if anyone else wanted prayer. A woman came forward who was experiencing terrible pain in her shoulder and neck area. As we prayed for her, God completely healed her, and she regained full movement in her shoulder and neck. Pain-free and with tears streaming down her face, she encountered the sweet presence of the Holy Spirit.

The Lord Your Healer

I was in a worship service, giving thanks and rejoicing in the Lord, when I received a tap on the shoulder. I turned around to catch the expectant glance of a teenage boy I had never met. He addressed me with all the faith in the world. "Mr. Brad, I want you to pray for my back because I believe Jesus will heal me if you do." I gladly laid my hand on his back and commanded the pain to leave while giving thanks to Jesus for the lad and for his incredible faith. A few minutes later, while the worship service was still going, I went over to the young man and asked him how his back felt. He told me with excitement in his voice, "I feel heat on my back and my back is not hurting at all!"

About three days later, I received word from this boy's mother. She informed me that her son had been having terrible back pain for over three weeks and after meeting with a doctor, the doctor had scheduled him to have X-rays done. He had been unable to participate in PE, he hadn't slept well, and he had been complaining for three weeks straight about the pain and discomfort in his back. However, after we met on that Sunday during worship his back was completely healed. For the past three days he had slept well and played sports with his friends, and the mother had not heard another word about the pain in his back. She happily reported to me that she canceled the X-rays because it was obvious to her after the three days, her son had been radically healed. The mother recently informed me that months later, she son was still completely pain-free without any complications.

I had a word of knowledge that God wanted to heal hips during a Tuesday night meeting. After sharing the gospel, I gave the word. Two people came for prayer. The first person, a man, told us his hip was hurting. We prayed for him but nothing happened, as he was still in pain. I asked him what exactly had happened to his hip. He told us that he had fallen earlier in the week and the pain had started then. It was beneficial to have this information, because now we were aware that his pain was from trauma. We prayed again, commanding a spirit of trauma to get out of his hip. Instantly, the pain left and he began to walk completely pain-free!

The second person, a woman, had severe arthritis in the hip. She told the people who prayed for her that her hip was throbbing even as she came to the front. She could barely walk down to the front because the pain was so severe. They prayed in Jesus' name and commanded arthritis to leave her hip. All the pain ceased instantly! What joy consumed the lady as she began to move around, completely free from arthritis after years of suffering. Exodus 15:26 is translated in our Bible as "I am the Lord who heals you."

I entered a church near my hometown to preach the gospel. As I preached about righteousness and sonship, I told the people in that place that because God was well-pleased to give us the kingdom (Luke 12:32), we were about to witness the power of God. I called a man to the front with knee problems and told him God was going to heal him. He had an injury from years earlier playing football. His wife and I prayed for him and God completely healed his knees. After this, we saw about ten more people healed of various infirmities.

One of my favorite miracles from this meeting was a young girl who was healed. She was about eleven years old and was wearing a brace on her hand because her finger was broken and bent. As she took off the brace, I called the other children to come over and command her finger to be healed. As the children prayed, the girl's finger completely straightened out. The young girl got super excited and yelled for her mother's attention. She showed her mom that her finger had just straightened out and there was no pain. As the young girl stared at me in amazement, she began to weep uncontrollably as the realization of what God had done for her sank in. Talk about a fun time! I was laughing and soaking up the goodness of our Father.

We saw several people with back pain healed in this service, as well as pain from a tumor healed in a young man. A few weeks after this meeting, I bumped into some of the people from this church and they were excited to tell me that they were still completely pain-free.

"Greater Works than These"

I love and believe in Jesus, the Son of God. If you believe in Him as well, then this promise from Jesus in John 14:12–14 is for you. Jesus states, "Most assuredly, I say to you, he who believes in Me, the works that I do he will do also; and greater works than these he will do, because I go to My Father. And whatever you ask in My name, that I will do, that the Father may be glorified in the Son. If you ask anything in My name, I will do it." Jesus healed, Jesus prophesied, Jesus cast out demons, and Jesus did many other works while preaching about the kingdom of heaven. Jesus commanded His disciples to do the same (Matthew 10:7–8). Before ascending to heaven after being raised from the dead, Jesus told His disciples to go and make more disciples just like them and to teach them to do the same things Jesus had commanded them to do (Matthew 28:18–20). Thank God Christianity is not powerless, and that Jesus is the same today as He was then (Hebrews 13:8).

While ministering one Friday night, I told the people listening that the Holy Spirit was about to give them words of knowledge that would reveal what He was wanting to heal. Roughly six different people got words of knowledge, and God showed up and healed many people. I believe between ten to fifteen different miracles happened Friday night, and I will share a few of them here.

My wife got a word of knowledge that God wanted to heal toes that had been smashed. A woman in attendance stood up, and her toes had been smashed that morning by a water heater. She could not wiggle her toes, and there was bruising. My wife prayed with her, commanding the pain to leave in Jesus' name. The woman immediately began to wiggle her toes around pain-free. She then removed her shoe and showed that all the bruising was gone. Her husband was dumbfounded because he saw the bruising earlier that day and knew she could not move her toes.

Another woman felt that God wanted to heal pain in the left shoulder. Two different people received prayer for this and were instantly healed. One lady could not lift her arm very much because of the pain and stiffness in her left shoulder. However, after prayer, she began to weep as she moved her shoulder and arm all the way over her head again and again with no pain. Another man got a word that God wanted to heal the lower part of the back. A lady immediately stood, saying that her lower back had really been bothering her for quite some time. As soon as the guy put his hand on her back, the pain left. Prayer was not needed, as the Holy Spirit healed her back at the touch. The woman's look of shock told me the pain had instantly left. She started grinning and saying, "It's completely well."

In addition to these miracles, knees were healed, foot problems were healed, and many people received prophetic words of encouragement and direction as well. What an amazing night in the presence of God as He flowed through many different people to heal and give prophetic words. All I did was teach and flow with the Holy Spirit, and He moved through the body of Christ. What a beautiful sight indeed.

I attended a Friday night worship service in Ashford, Alabama, with a church family. We were just there to worship Jesus and meet some new people. We only knew the man who had invited us to this service. Before I left home, I asked the Holy Spirit if there was anything He wanted to share with me about the service. He briefly showed me a picture in my heart of a lady with dark hair in her late forties or early fifties. He told me she was having numbness in her left shoulder and down her left arm going into her hand. He wanted to heal her.

Before I addressed the people at the end of the service, I pointed out to the church family the lady that God was going to heal. After sharing this information and while the pastor was closing out the service, I went over to the man who had invited us and told him I believed God wanted to heal people. He allowed me to speak for a moment. I told the people that God wanted to heal a lady with numbness in her left shoulder and arm that went down into her hand. There were only about forty people total in attendance.

Sure enough, the exact lady who I told the church family would respond to the word stood up. It was the same lady the Holy Spirit had showed me before the service that night. She did indeed have numbness that started in her left shoulder and went down her arm and into her hand. She was completely healed. Words of knowledge (1 Corinthians 12:8) are so much fun. Also, Jesus said in John 10:27 that His sheep hear and obey His voice. I love the fact that by faith we can hear God whisper instruction to our heart.

We have the great privilege of having the God of all creation make His home inside of us. We get to teach and demonstrate His kingdom on this Earth. In Matthew 10:7–8, Jesus commands His disciples to teach about the kingdom of heaven being at hand. After they teach, they are to demonstrate the kingdom in power as Jesus commanded. In Luke chapter 10, Jesus commands the disciples to demonstrate the kingdom of heaven by healing the sick. After they demonstrate the power of God, Jesus then commands them to teach about the kingdom.

As Jesus' disciples, we have the same commission to teach and demonstrate the kingdom of heaven in power. Empowered with this same commission, I taught one Sunday morning at my home church about the kingdom of heaven. After teaching, I gave our congregation the opportunity to demonstrate His kingdom being at hand in power. We asked people to raise their hands if they had physical problems that they wanted God to heal. Then the people around them found out what the problem was with the individual for whom they were praying. After giving God thanks for the finished work of Christ, they commanded the ailments to leave in Jesus' name. After a brief prayer, we had them test out their bodies to see if God had made them whole. I had people raise their hand if God had just absolutely and completely healed their body. At least eleven people raised their hands.

Once, while speaking at my home church, I declared several things that God was about to heal. One of those words was "diabetes." When I declared God was healing diabetes, a precious lady who I know very well stood to her feet. No one prayed for her and no one touched her, but Jesus absolutely did. She has been diabetic for over seven years. Normal blood sugar levels range between 80 and 120; in the mornings, however, her levels were never below 300. She had been on medication for the past seven years and for quite some time had been required to take insulin.

The following morning, after she stood in faith that God was healing her of diabetes, she checked her blood sugar. To her great wonder and awe, her number was eighty-nine. She made the decision to skip her medication for the first time in over seven years. At lunch that same day, she ate her normal meal but had sweet tea and two fig bars with her food. She checked her blood sugar again and it was 103. Again, the next morning, her number was in the normal range at 107. The next Sunday, a full week from when God healed her, she stood in front of the church and shared her incredible testimony. She had been a full week with her blood sugar numbers in the normal range and had not taken any more medication or insulin. God had completely healed her of diabetes.

The Goodness of God

I believe we have entered a time when the goodness of God will be seen by all. He hasn't changed, but we are entering a time when all people, Christian or not, are having their awareness shifted into a place where it is impossible to see God as anything other than good. His goodness knows no bounds.

At a recent church meeting, there were a couple of college students in attendance. One of them had a bulging disc in her back that was causing severe discomfort and pain. I told her friend she should put her hand on her friend's back and pray for her. The young lady didn't believe God would heal her friend through her, but I told her He would. She listened to me and prayed for her friend, commanding the pain to leave and for the disc to go back into place in Jesus' name. As she did, the young lady she was praying for began to cry as the presence and power of God came upon her. She began to move her torso around and bend in place. Sure enough, God had completely healed the bulging disc in her back. The young lady that prayed for her just began to cry when she realized God had flowed through her to heal her friend.

During worship time on a Sunday morning, the Holy Spirit told me He wanted to heal left shoulders. I went up to the pastor and relayed this information. He called the word out, and multiple people raised their hands stating they were having problems with their left shoulder. They discovered after brief prayer that their shoulders had been instantly healed.

During prayer time, the Lord spoke to me and said He wanted to do extraordinary miracles in a service I was holding that night. I asked Him specifically what He wanted to do. The Lord told me He wanted to restructure people's DNA. As the meeting began, I told the people what the Lord had just told me, declaring into the microphone that He was going to restructure people's DNA.

A young lady in her mid-twenties came off the worship stage a few moments later. She looked at me and said, "Brad, my throat feels like it is on fire. What is happening to me?" I told her the Lord was healing her. I then asked what had been ailing her. She had been diagnosed with Hashimoto's disease, which affects the thyroid. She was taking several medications to help with symptoms. She would have severe headaches and did not do well with bright light, among other things. After this encounter with God, she stopped taking her medications. A few days later, her mom was even shocked by how well she was doing. It has been over eight months, and still the young lady has no symptoms. God completely healed her of Hashimoto's disease.

A few weeks later, the Lord told me before a meeting that He wanted to heal hearing problems. I called the word out in the meeting, which a young military man was visiting. His ear began to burn, and his mother came to get me. This young man was in tears as the presence of God was on him. He had seventy percent hearing loss in that ear from an injury in the military; however, on this night, God opened his ear and completely healed him. He could hear just as well from the injured ear as he could out of his good ear.

Chapter 6: Crusades in South America

I have had the wonderful opportunity to visit the nation of Peru several times to preach the gospel. On my first trip there, I saw many miracles and many people give their life to Jesus. But I want to tell you about my favorite part of our two-week trip. One day we decided to go into the slums in Iquitos, Peru. We wanted to find some children and just love them like Jesus does.

Our interpreter and friend, Pablo Arimborgo, went with Jimmy Hornsby and me. The living conditions in these places were horrific. Trash, disease, and poverty were rampant in the places we visited. We saw several groups of kids playing with some marbles in the dirt. We were able to find a little candy shack set up in this poor neighborhood, so we struck up a conversation with some of the kids and asked them how to play their game of marbles. After several minutes of talking with these precious children, we led a few of them over to the candy shack with us. We began to buy them snacks, candy, and their favorite drink. It looked like Christmastime as these children were so excited to be given these small gifts. As their screams of joy were heard throughout the area, more and more children began coming up to the candy shop to see what was going on. It was truly amazing to see the sheer excitement and thankfulness exhibited by these young children, ranging in age from two to ten years old. We just loved on these children, expecting nothing in return.

I could feel the heart of Jesus so strongly for these children that I began to cry as an overwhelming sense of the love of God flowed into my heart. His presence was amazing as we hung out with these children. After spending close to an hour with them, we shared with them why Jimmy and I had come to their country. We briefly told them about Jesus and how much He loves them. After a couple minutes of sharing the gospel of Jesus, we asked them if they wanted to ask Jesus into their hearts. Every single one of those kids—which was around twenty-five of them—accepted Jesus into their heart, praise God. How the angels in heaven rejoiced with us as these children asked Jesus to be Lord of their lives (Luke 15:10).

What would our cities look like if we allowed God to flow through each one of us so that we became radical love to all people around us? Is it possible for us to love people with all their unique personalities and gifts, as well as their faults without holding their sins against them? I believe so. Luke 6:35–36: "But love your enemies, do good, and lend, hoping for nothing in return; and your reward will be great, and you will be sons of the Most High. For He is kind to the unthankful and evil. Therefore, be merciful, just as your Father also is merciful." I ask God to help me be free so I am able to love and encourage everyone around me to know God. "Unto the upright there arises light in the darkness; He is gracious, and full of compassion, and righteous... He has dispersed abroad, He has given to the poor; His righteousness endures forever; His horn will be exalted with honor" (Psalm 112:4, 9). "He who has pity on the poor lends to the Lord, And He will pay back what he has given" (Proverbs 19:17).We all have the ability to love the poor and those less fortunate.

Miracles in the Park

Later, in my first trip to Peru, Jimmy and I met a woman in a wheelchair at a park where evangelist Steve Fatow had just preached.

We began to pray with the sick. When we laid hands on this woman, the power of God literally began to shake her in the seat. She began to weep uncontrollably and the power of God upon her was so intense, it truly felt tangible. She began to vibrate wildly in her wheelchair, as heart-stirring screams came flowing from her mouth. This lasted for about five minutes. The lady's children and grandchildren were with her.

One woman, who spoke Spanish and English, talked to me about the lady for a minute. She told me that the lady I was praying for had had a stroke six months earlier and could not walk; she had no strength in her legs and was confined to the wheelchair. I then told the lady that she was going to walk, turned to the woman in the wheelchair, and instructed her to grab my hand. She was probably in her sixties and very heavy.

When she grabbed my hand, she came up out of that wheelchair, praise God. She began to walk with me and people all over the place were shouting "Jesus" in Spanish. The power of God was so strong and the joy of the Lord that I was experiencing with this family was truly mind-blowing. I walked with this lady for a minute, holding her hand. Then I felt the lady began to slap at my hand: she wanted to walk by herself. When this happened, the lady began to walk perfectly with no wobble at all—perfectly normal steps. This went on for a while and complete pandemonium ensued.

People were worshipping God and miracles began to break out all over the place. One eight-year-old girl behind us who was completely blind in one eye was healed. We had reports of lots of other miracles happening on this night in the park.

But back to the lady who was in the wheelchair. After about twenty minutes of walking all over the place, she placed two of her grandchildren in the wheelchair for a fun ride and we watched her push the wheelchair that she had been in for the past six months home herself.

On another visit to Peru with Jimmy and Steve Fatow, we traveled to Pisco, Peru, to preach the gospel under the stars. We saw many hundreds of precious people give their lives to Jesus in the three nights we were there. The blind saw, the deaf had their ears opened, and the lame walked. On the third night of the campaign, we had six people give testimony that they had been healed of blindness.

In addition to these, we had a lovely young girl, under ten years old, receive her hearing. She was born deaf in one of her ears. Her family testified that her deaf ear became completely opened and she could hear words and sounds out of that ear for the first time in her life.

The Raw Power of God

On the first night of the campaign, they wheeled an elderly lady up to the front in a wheelchair. It was obvious that walking was not a part of her life anymore. However, Jesus had other plans for her.

I walked over to her, and yelled for strength to flow into her body. I commanded her legs to work properly in Jesus' name, and I told paralysis to leave her body. Next, I grabbed her hands and snatched her up out of that wheelchair. She held onto my hands and stumbled a few feet. After traveling a few more feet, I let go of her hands and she was walking unaided by human hands. People erupted into shouts of praise to Jesus as they watched this precious lady, known throughout their community, as she received her miracle from Jesus and walked perfectly normal.

We also saw tumors shrivel and totally disappear. One lady and her husband shared that the wife had a tumor of twenty years. It disappeared as she was totally healed. Another lady with a tumor for five years got healed and the tumor completely left her body. Many, many other miracles took place. We saw a cab driver weep under the power of God as he gave his life to Jesus after dropping us off at our hotel. We watched as two waitresses surrendered their life to Jesus as we shared the gospel with them.

On another occasion, I had the great privilege to travel to the Dominican Republic to preach the gospel in an open-air crusade in the city of Cabrera with Steve Fatow. We witnessed the power of God raise another woman out of a wheelchair. This was the third time I had witnessed this happen. She walked as people worshipped Jesus and was able to go up the stairs on the stage as others lifted the empty wheelchair up on stage as well. Another lady testified through streams of tears and laughter of how Jesus had just restored sight in her blind eye. Another lady gave testimony with great enthusiasm about how she felt heat moving through her deaf ear. The next thing she knew, her ear popped open and she could hear completely out of that previously deaf ear.

A man gave testimony with his family standing beside him. They were all ecstatically praising Jesus because his back and leg had just been completely healed. A few days earlier, this man had been attacked maliciously by several men with sticks. They had beaten him and severely damaged some of the vertebrae in his back, so he had a terrible limp. However, as we began to pray the family heard sounds of bones cracking and saw their family member getting blasted by the raw power of God as his back was fused back together. The severe limp he had was gone. He did back bends and jumped up and down on the stage, completely pain-free.

Another woman who was mute had her speech return, and she began to utter praises to Jesus. Multiple people had tumors completely dissolve as the Holy Spirit healed them. Many people surrendered their lives and hearts to the Lord Jesus. So many people were healed over our three nights there that we couldn't even began to count or record all the miracles Jesus did. Each night hundreds of people were healed and rejoiced in the presence of Jesus. Addicts were healed and delivered. Mental disorders were eradicated.

Conclusion

There was a time in each of our lives when we looked at life through the eyes of a child, when anything and everything was possible—when the word *impossible* did not exist. I pray my story gives you a glimpse of what is possible when you walk in faith and believe for the impossible.

As you begin your journey into your own uncharted waters, lean on God's promises and not on your own understanding. You will begin to see how a supernatural lifestyle is available to all of God's children.

Jesus told us that everyone who believes in Him will do the same works He has done and greater. You are the temple of the Holy Spirit. A supernatural lifestyle is available because of the Holy Spirit's indwelling. Each of us is equipped once we are born again to see the kingdom.

Each day on life's journey is filled with opportunities for us to step out in faith, expecting His world to collide with this world. Dare to believe that Christ in you is the hope of glory. You are filled with His glory, and people are eagerly waiting to experience Jesus' love and healing through you!

About the Author

The Lord rescued Brad Bonner from a life of darkness and despair in 2010 and set him on a path of discovery. Alongside him on this journey are his loving wife of thirteen years, April, and their three precious girls: Cadance, Gabby, and London. Brad and April are full-time pastors at The Gathering Place in Donalsonville, Georgia; they also minister the gospel in South America.

Brad can be contacted at goautigers85@yahoo.com.

We are a Christian-based publishing company that was founded in 2009. Our primary focus has been to establish authors.

"5 Fold Media was the launching partner that I needed to bring *The Transformed Life* into reality. This team worked diligently and with integrity to help me bring my words and vision into manifestation through a book that I am proud of and continues to help people and churches around the world. None of this would have been possible without the partnership and education I received from 5 Fold Media."

- Pastor John Carter, Lead Pastor of Abundant Life Christian Center, Syracuse, NY, Author and Fox News Contributor

**The Transformed Life* is foreworded by Pastor A.R. Bernard, received endorsements from best-selling authors Phil Cooke, Rick Renner, and Tony Cooke, and has been featured on television shows such as TBN and local networks.

5 Fold Media
5701 E. Circle Dr. #338, Cicero, NY 13039
manuscript@5foldmedia.com

Find us on Facebook, Twitter, and YouTube.

Discover more at www.5FoldMedia.com.

CPSIA information can be obtained
at www.ICGtesting.com
Printed in the USA
FSHW02n0741170518

9 781942 056744